PRINCIPLES

O F

PASTORAL SUCCESS

Richard S. Taylor

FRANCIS ASBURY PRESS
of Zondervan Publishing House
Grand Rapids, Michigan

Principles of Pastoral Success
Copyright © 1989 by Richard S. Taylor

Francis Asbury Press is an imprint of Zondervan Publishing House,
1415 Lake Drive, S.E., Grand Rapids, Michigan 49506.

Library of Congress Cataloging in Publication Data

Taylor, Richard Shelley, 1912–
    Principles of pastoral success.
    Bibliography: p.
    1. Clergy—Office. 2. Pastoral theology.
    I. Title.
    BV660.2.T39   1989   253'.2   88-35071
    ISBN 0-310-75401-1

Edited by Robert D. Wood

Printed in the United States of America

89 90 91 92 93 94 / ML / 10 9 8 7 6 5 4 3 2 1

To
BERTHA
Whose companionship is God's gift

David's Word to Solomon

"Now, my son, the LORD be with you, and may you have success and build the house of the LORD your God, as he said you would. May the LORD give you discretion and understanding when he puts you in command over Israel, so that you may keep the law of the LORD your God. Then you will have success if you are careful to observe the decrees and laws that the LORD gave Moses for Israel. Be strong and courageous. Do not be afraid or discouraged."

1 Chronicles 22:11–13

CONTENTS

PREFACE

For well over half a century my favorite people have been preachers. I feel their pains and frustrations. I sense when they are nervous in the pulpit, or are in the brush, and empathize with them; I have been there too many times myself. I have a well-working radar which picks up signals of stress in the pastorate.

My credentials include being the son of a preacher, pastoring twenty years myself, working with pastors in hundreds of revivals, observing them and fraternizing with them in camp meetings, preachers' retreats (in many cases as the speaker), district activities, conferences and assemblies, and spending a total of twenty-five years in the classroom teaching budding theologues, including an overlapping three years as associate in the department of education and ministry of my denomination. During this period, I supervised the reorganization of the denomination's educational program for licensed ministers.

I have been deeply distressed when pastors flounder. I have seen men leave the ministry for needless reasons. They could have made it, but they didn't. I have seen others plod on courageously, but performing far below their potential.

For much of my more mature life I have been gripped by a yearning to help preachers, especially pastors. This was my drive in editing *The Nazarene Pastor* (now *The Preacher's Magazine*) for eight and a half years. This was my aim in writing *Preaching Holiness Today*. And this is equally my motive in writing this book.

The book represents the insights accumulated across these years of personal experience and observation. As such it is not a scholarly research study. Most of the illustrations are straight out of life—the pastoral life, seen or known firsthand. In fact, in a few cases, pastors may recognize themselves, though I hope the identity will not be obvious to others. If any such anecdote brings personal embarrassment to the reader, I can only beg indulgence, reassure him or her of my goodwill, and hope that the benefit to others will justify my liberty.

This book is designed to help pastors in their own private war on mediocrity. It is written to aid pastors to be all they can be and are meant by God to be. It will be of little interest to pastors who do not wish to improve or see need for improvement. But it may bring new hope and guidance to pastors who know their output for God is less than their potential and who are looking for insights which could help them understand and remedy the problem.

There are three groups of preachers I especially have in mind. First, I would like to condition the thinking of the prospective pastor before he takes his first church. Second, I would like to make available some insights which could steady the course of men in the early years of their ministry. Third, perhaps I dare hope that this book may reinvigorate pastors in mid-life. Many need a fresh infusion of enthusiasm, a renewed commitment, and even more urgently, some midcourse corrections which will enable them to make their middle and later years their most productive and satisfying.

The emphasis of this book is not on techniques but on principles. Many details of "know-how" must be sought for elsewhere. But if principles of the pastoral ministry are grasped and become the molding and directing force of one's professional life, the techniques can be acquired and will then have value. Without observing principles the pastor will be vainly—though perhaps expertly—"beating the air." To change the figure: A superstructure built on false and insecure foundations will collapse, and the higher and more elaborate the structure, the greater will be the crash.

Both positive and negative modes of discussion are in these chapters. Both are needed; therefore, no apology is required. Let us hope that the final effect will be all positive.

Richard S. Taylor
Portland, Oregon
1988

1

SUCCESS IN THE MINISTRY

No man or woman called of God to the pastoral ministry plans to fail. The desire is to succeed in the eyes of leaders, people, family—and most of all in the eyes of God. And God has planned for us to succeed. A call to the pastoral ministry is an assurance that God sees the potential for success. As Ethel Waters used to say, "God don't make no flops."

Yet some do fail. In some cases they fail in their first pastorate—but succeed thereafter. Some fail in their first and second and third—and by this time they are "out." Some struggle with a level of success which in the light of their potential is itself a failure. Others fail to round out a full lifetime of ministry and drop out years before they are of retirement age.

Causes of failure are really not many. They are weaknesses in a few critical areas, which could have been corrected. A chapter in this book will be devoted to identifying these. More frequently the cause of failure is an attention to superstructures to the neglect of foundations. The underlying principles of the ministry have not been learned.

DEFINING SUCCESS SOUNDLY

The first principle is the imperative of entering the ministry with a biblical philosophy of success. Some pastors' concepts of success are unrealistic. They are shaped by the big dramatic success story of some superchurch that has grown from a membership of seventeen to two thousand in four years. With such yardsticks the vast majority of pastors will be struggling under a sense of failure, even guilt, all their lives. There is nothing worse than the tyranny of a false measure of success. To be inspired by what others do is good, but to be intimidated by it is paralyzing, especially if the example becomes a standard by which our ministry is denigrated.

Let us begin, then, with a Christian mind-set. Since the ministry is a service profession, success must be related to effective service. Since the ministry works with people at the cutting edge of life, and deals with invisible and intangible realities, success cannot be quantified in terms of sales or balance sheets. The pastor is stretched upon a cross of heaven-and-earth tensions that are staggering in their eternal issues. For him there is a cosmic dimension in this word *success,* of which the secular world knows nothing. His wares are God, the gospel, and eternal souls.

Furthermore the pastor is just one in a vast interplay of spiritual forces, including the whole of Christendom and reaching back to the Cross and beyond. He builds on other men's labors. Jesus said to his disciples, "I sent you to reap what you have not worked for. Others have done the hard work, and you have reaped the benefits of their labor" (John 4:38). In no calling therefore is humility more appropriate than in the pastorate, and in no calling is pride more odious.

Because the pastor is God's servant, not his own, he

cannot selfishly angle for position. He knows that he cannot be *promoted* from the center of God's will. His Christian scale of values assures him that there are no "unimportant" churches, any more than there are "unimportant" people. We dare not become pagans by measuring success in terms of "moving up" to a bigger church or "moving down" to a smaller. As Jesus would say, that is the way the Gentiles think.

And the most obnoxious poison is cynicism about this. Of course there are human dimensions as well as divine, and of course there are blunders and inequities. Many things happen in the ministry which are not fair, but neither was the Cross. A Christian is one who believes that God is greater than man and conducts himself accordingly. Let the pastor be a Christian. Only as a Christian, with a thoroughly renewed mind (Rom. 12:2), will he be able to think straight about success.

THE DIMENSIONS OF SUCCESS

There is a quantitative dimension to success, but other dimensions are interlocked with it in such a way that the quantitative finds its true meaning and validity in them.

The spiritual dimension

Success in this dimension is the most difficult of all. But the pastoral ministry finds its crux right here. Peter was commissioned: "Feed my sheep" (John 21:17). Years later Peter himself exhorted, "Be shepherds of God's flock" (1 Peter 5:2). Having a church so large that the pastor must operate as a "rancher" is a false mark of success, if being a "rancher" means he feels he has graduated from the need to be a shepherd.

Sheep and shepherding are alien concepts to twentieth-century urban sophisticates. We are much more at home with the concepts of promotion and management. Yet the pastor who is a great manager but aloof from his people, and who does not teach and nurture them in their spiritual life, is not a success but a failure at the level of his primary obligation.

A pastor who leaves behind a spiritually healthy congregation when he moves to another charge has passed the most fundamental test of success. Under his ministry there should have been a growth in the sturdiness of his people's walk with the Lord and a development in their understanding of truth. Their grasp of the Scriptures should be more mature than when he first began to serve them. They should be more resistant to the spiritual diseases of occultism on the outside of the church and carnal strife on the inside. They should manifest a growing capacity for unselfish, outgoing service, and a deepening concern for the salvation of souls. Faithful and joyous stewardship should be a way of life.

Basically this spiritual dimension of success includes the pastor's skill in leading his people into full heart holiness and helping them to become established therein. A truly Pauline pastor will share Paul's passionate concern for the entire sanctification and preservation of his people (1 Thess. 3:10; 4:3–8; 5:23–24).

But experiencing the blessing is not enough. A concerned pastor will not be content until his people are so well indoctrinated in the concepts of full salvation that they can testify clearly and learn to articulate their beliefs to others, thus multiplying the pastor's ministry.

What kind of a person is apt to succeed in the spiritual dimension of ministry? He or she will exhibit four marks:

1. *Saintliness.* P. T. Forsyth said, "My first obligation to my people is my own sanctity." A pastor must model holiness. His people must see in him Christlikeness of

spirit and motive, in all places and circumstances. He must be a growing Christian. His personality should exhibit the joy of the Lord. A pastor should pray earnestly to be like Paul in his ability to say, "Imitate me" (1 Cor. 4:16).

2. *Understanding.* The pastor needs to understand the Bible, Christian doctrine, and people. To acquire such understanding he or she will have to be a thinker, an observer, and an avid student. He should read until he is theologically knowledgeable, and live in the Bible until, in the apt words of Forsyth, he can "wear it like a glove." His success in the spiritual dimension of the pastorate will be determined by his degree of competence in these three areas.

3. *Teaching ability.* This is a biblical requirement (1 Tim. 3:2; 2 Tim. 2:24). If a pastor would succeed he must learn to articulate truth clearly and effectively, both in the pulpit and out of the pulpit. His sermons should inform and edify as well as inspire. But his teaching should not be confined to preaching. A substantial portion of his total program should be devoted to discipling. When his church becomes too large for him to do it all himself, he must train laymen to do it or employ professionals who can. At this point the concept of "rancher" makes sense.

A one-track evangelistic style can militate against success as a teaching pastor. In one of my early pastorates I preached urgent evangelistic and searching sermons morning and night. One day a "mother in Israel" said gently, "Can't you give us an orange once in a while?" Only gradually did her meaning dawn on me. It was a turning point in my pastoral ministry. She was pleading for nourishment. And please, let it be a sweet orange rather than sour.

4. *Wisdom.* Some pastors are walking encyclopedias of academic knowledge—even psychological theory—but

they are not wise. Wisdom involves pedagogical skills. It also perceives where people are in their spiritual journey and the kind of care they need at this point. Wisdom exposes people to the right books and the right speakers. It knows when to confront and when to confirm. Better yet, it knows how to make even the confronting confirming.

The denominational yardstick

While some churches are independent, most belong loosely or closely to a denomination. In this relationship they have obligations to other components of the system. Their obligations are financial, for one thing, and involve missionary budgets, perhaps educational or other types of commitments. A denominational relationship not only imposes obligations but limitations. Most denominations have a "discipline" by which some degree of moral, doctrinal, and structural control is exercised in the interest of unity and strength.

It is a poor brand of ministerial success which operates as an island rather than part of the mainland. A pastor should be big enough to work comfortably with the whole field and teach his people to do the same. If he is small-minded and afflicted with "localitis" and, worse yet, "egoitis," his people will shrink in vision and shrivel in soul along with their leader. Selfish indifference to obligations outside of one's immediate circle is self-defeating, for the ultimate result cannot but be stagnation— spiritually, financially, and numerically. The spring of generous giving which is walled in from others will eventually dry up even for the local church.

A successful pastor builds a world consciousness into his people. He educates them in the ethos and programs of the entire denomination. By example he inspires delight in being a part of zone, district, and general activities. A sense of fraternity and loyalty—even church pride—is properly encouraged. Church periodicals will be seen on family reading tables. Missionary books will be read. Awareness of far-flung church enterprises will be increased, and the people will share in the victories elsewhere. Missionaries will be frequent guest speakers, sparking warm personal ties and inducing a deeper ministry of intercession.

The result will be an informed, involved, cooperative, enthusiastic laity, with horizons beyond the local church. They will be larger in soul. Budgets, rallies, assemblies or conferences, superintendents, mission fields, publishing houses, schools and colleges, will all seem like friends and be embraced in the broadening prayer-bonds of growing Christians.

In no aspect of church life will the adage be more fully demonstrated—"like priest, like people." A big-minded, world-visioned, leadership-respecting, budget-paying pastor will just naturally produce this kind of people. If he is a booster, they will be. But the rewards will be sweet; for if he boosts those above him, those below will boost him because they will catch his spirit. Magnanimity begets magnanimity.

The material dimension

At this point our concept of success must be expanded to cover the whole gamut of the modern pastor's functions. He is not only a preacher and teacher, not only a liturgist; but he is the legal head of a corporation. As such he is a planner, promoter, organizer, manager, advertiser, delegator, supervisor, and diplomat. Success in the pastoral ministry requires some degree of skill in every function.

Managing the physical and financial side of the church has been the Waterloo of many a pastor. Large churches have business managers, but approximately eighty-nine percent of Protestant churches in North America have an average Sunday morning attendance of 225 or less (Lyle Schaller). The great majority of them cannot afford full-time business managers. The responsibility therefore in most cases is squarely on the pastor's shoulders.

Great sermons will not compensate for unpaid bills. Fervent piety will not cancel the bad impression of peeling paint. The first church of one seminary graduate was near a secular college. Hundreds of students walked by the property every day. Friends had expected this brilliant student and strong preacher soon to pack the church. But the pews remained unfilled. Neighbors and students couldn't get past the uncut grass, neglected shrubs, and the ragged, sagging sign, "Jesus is the Answer." The brilliant seminarian did not last long there. Someone failed to tell him that property preaches also.

Not only must property be maintained, but a way must be found to pay the pastor and staff, to pay local accounts promptly and honorably, and to discharge faithfully the obligations of the church to the various entities of the denomination. Everything is at stake— credit, reputation, influence, the honor of Christ, souls. Methods cannot be discussed here. A smart pastor can always learn how to get a handle on finance in harmony with the procedures and restrictions of his own church.

What kind of man is most apt to succeed in this area of the ministry? Fundamentally it will be one who has a very high sense of personal responsibility and a keen awareness of the priority such matters claim in the integrity of the work. If he has a business background or a natural aptitude in practical management, so much the better. But at the very least his IQ needs the ballast of common sense. Some of us who by temperament are "eggheads" and hardly know the business end of a hammer, will have a rougher time, but the obligation is equally upon us. As a beginner I wanted to take my ministry out in praying, studying, preaching, and as little calling as I could get away with. Administration I abominated. But I soon learned that that also was my job, and I learned that if I organized carefully, planned far enough ahead, and enlisted others wisely, I could do it. I even learned to enjoy it.

INCLUDING CHURCH GROWTH

What is church growth? Fundamentally it is the increase of regular born-again attenders in the regular services, validated as authentic church growth by their active participation in the life of the church. True church growth is more than the aggregation of the unsaved, it is the growth of the kingdom of God, consisting of men and women and boys and girls who have been brought to Christ. As such, it is the kind of growth which has a built-in impetus toward further growth. If this enlargement is sound and well-managed, it will reflect itself in membership statistics. But a swollen membership roll in and of itself does not prove healthy church growth. Some churches keep adding names to the roll, but new members drift or move away, and the actual attendance and participation remain static.

In pushing church growth we must avoid the grave peril of making it an end in itself. We can learn from the remark of Henry Ford: "Try to run a business solely to make money and the business will die."[1] Making money, he insisted, should be a by-product of providing a service. The service must always be kept center stage. Likewise, in the pastor's mind the simple task of winning men to Christ, teaching them to live holy and useful lives, and finally get to heaven, should be the unshifting focus. His success in doing this will spell church growth. But if his focus is on church growth per se, he will inevitably measure the importance of this or that prospect not in the light of his own eternal need but in the light of his potential as a church growth asset. This mania—as it can easily become—will tend to dictate methodology, with the result that the church growth he succeeds in achieving may not be church growth with integrity.

Nevertheless, real church growth, as properly defined, should be the normal expectation. A pastor should have no intention less than reaching the lost for Christ and bringing them into the church. Any other plan will mean a dwarfed ministry and a stunted church. There is something defective in a pastor's godliness if he is content with zero growth. For at the heart of true godliness is a love for souls, not only the sheep in the flock, but the lost sheep, and the potential sheep, for whom Christ died, and who so desperately need the Savior.

It is true that bald statistics can never measure the undercurrents of the kingdom of God. Well known is the story of the couple in Louisiana who saved their money to bring a prominent evangelist to their community, expecting to have a great revival. Only one fourteen-year-old boy was converted. Outwardly the effort seemed like a failure. But that boy was Roy T. Williams, who became one of the great holiness leaders of this century. The real success of that meeting should be counted not as a mere *one* but a multitude.

Furthermore, no pastor's success should be evaluated by the occasional statistical reversal. Economic upheavals can decimate whole communities, reducing church rolls as well as population. Epidemics or weather can play havoc with attendance records. An honest clean-up of the membership roll (perhaps removing names of persons long since dead or long since moved away with whereabouts unknown) can result in a net loss, even though new members have been received. Such a loss is a credibility gain, but it will not show on the records.

It is also true that some churches have less potential for growth than others. This may be due to external conditions over which the church has no control, as in the case of a radically changing neighborhood or perhaps a disappearing population. "Growth potential," observes C. Peter Wagner of such churches, "is near zero." Then he mercifully adds, "Churches with terminal illnesses do not need to be loaded with more guilt because they are not growing; they need to be cared for and counseled."[2] And some noble soul needs to shepherd them without being made to feel inferior.

Another kind of external condition which impedes growth is a location which serves a highly mobile population, as in a military or college community or even in an inner-city mission setting. As Wagner says, "Many of these churches have excellent outreach programs; they are leading large numbers of unbelievers to Jesus Christ and folding them into the church, but year after year the church just stays about the same."[3] This is real growth in the kingdom, recorded fully and joyfully in heaven. But these churches will never make good illustrations for books on church growth. This may help us avoid a tunnel-vision approach to the whole matter of church growth—defining it *exclusively* in terms of statistical enlargement.

But by far the most prevalent impediment to church growth is lack of motivation. The potential is present but the desire is not. Such churches are content with their size as they are. Wagner speaks of them as "single-cell." Lyle E. Schaller calls them "fellowships," and likens them to cats with their nine lives and benign independence.[4] Members of these fellowships actually prefer the comfortable security and intimacy of a small church. Too many outsiders make them uneasy. This may be a normal sociological trait, but it also constitutes a spiritual problem, for such churches enjoy themselves in selfish indifference to the unsaved and unchurched all around them. A pastor of such a church needs to understand the psychology at work here—and be part of the family—yet never succumb to it. He should be forever leaning against it, seeking to awaken his people to a vision which sees beyond their own pew.

Hence numerical growth as a criterion of success includes more than a bare increase in membership and attendance. It includes the successful inculcation of a passion for soul winning in the congregation. The mood of complacency needs to be replaced by the excitement of outreach. Part of pastoral success is one's skill in turning the attention of his people outward until they become imbued with the understanding that we are saved to save others. Even preaching holiness should be a means of deepening and cleansing the church for its mission of evangelism. A sanctified church will reach more people for Christ than a carnal, worldly-minded church. The supposed "power" of a professed Spirit-filled life is spurious if at its heart is not the power for witnessing which Jesus promised (Acts 1:8).

What kind of a pastor will most likely have a growing church? First, he will have staying power. He will stay long enough to earn the right to lead. Second, he will succeed in awakening in his people enthusiasm for growth. Third, he will lead them to mobilize their resources for evangelism. Fourth, he will know how through discipling and assimilating to consolidate his gains.

This will be easier for some persons than others. The pastor who temperamentally is a shepherd at heart and loves the quiet pace and the human relationships of a family-style church will not do so well as the pastor who by temperament is a task-oriented, dominating leader.

Probably Timothy was the first kind; nevertheless Paul admonished him, "Do the work of an evangelist" (2 Tim. 4:5). While there is a limit to which we can expect a square peg to learn to fit into a round hole, and we must acknowledge and *respect* different pastoral types, no one should be encouraged to excuse himself from winning at least one person to Jesus in a year's time and bringing him into the church. Even the shyest preacher can do at least that much if he prays enough, puts his mind to the task, and goes at it in desperate earnestness. His church growth may not equal another's, but it will be better than stagnation.

Finally, church growth in any degree presupposes the necessity of learning the principles and skills necessary to success. Perhaps the following chapters can aid the pastor-reader in this achievement.

2

QUALITIES OF SUCCESSFUL PASTORS

Certain qualities are almost universally found in pastors who are highly successful (and whose success is bona fide in God's sight). Perhaps the following can serve as a benchmark for self-study.[1]

QUALITIES OF PROFESSIONAL PROFICIENCY

Intensity

No pastor will do more than limp through his ministerial life who is overly solicitous about his comforts and pleasures. The man who succeeds in this day is the man with a one-track mind. His enthusiasm for the ministry is so strong and steady that he feels no need to find secondary excitements to make life interesting. To him nothing could possibly be so fascinating as his everyday work as a pastor. The satisfaction of being a pastor is infinitely deeper and more rewarding than that of a good golf score. Hobbies that would keep him from his people hold little interest for him. He knows nothing of emotional boredom. Some pastors take too many days off and too many trips for them ever to enjoy large success in the ministry. In some cases their observing laymen wonder what they are resting from (or *running* from?).

The man who succeeds is about half-crazy in his determination to win souls, care for his flock, and build his church. His people, his sermons, his plans, his problems consume his attention day and night. His work dominates his conversation—as his wife very well knows.

This intensity should not be confused with tension. Pastors may be intense without being uptight. Up-tightness kills. Such persons "break down not because they are run-down but because they are wound-up." A joyous spirit with plenty of laughter is not incompatible with the kind of intensity which marks the successful pastor.

Energy

To give oneself to the ministry with that dedication which the work demands requires a high level of physical energy. The very nature of the work makes it emotionally and physically draining. Counseling, calling, praying, preaching are high-energy activities. If one is fatigued when counseling, the counselee may get the impression of disinterest. As for preaching, sermons flounder when energy flags. And an exhausted pastor is in no state to conduct board or council meetings.

Some pastors are blessed with seemingly endless reserves of physical energy. They can follow hours at their desk with hours at the hospital and further hours in business meetings and then on Sunday preach with drive and verve. In all the functions of the week their enthusiasm and warmth never seem to flag. They are alive and buoyant. They thrive on work. The pace is a tonic to them.

The danger these persons face is presumption. The adage that a candle burned at both ends is consumed twice as fast may be trite but it is still true. If these men and women do not build into their lifestyle some checks and balances, some ways of daily and weekly renewal, they are in danger of peaking too soon. It is sad when a man begins to drag and finds his energy sputtering just when in mid-life he should be at the zenith of his powers. For a few years the pastor may have had phenomenal success, but suddenly he or she is burned out.

Some pastors are handicapped with a chronic energy shortage from youth. This may be the legacy of an illness or it may be congenital; regardless of the reason, everything they do is a struggle. After preaching they are almost too exhausted to greet the people. Frequent days of rest, perhaps even in bed, are a necessity. Some strenuous activities normally enjoyed by other preachers must be avoided. There will always be those who say that the cure is more exercise, not less. In some cases this may be true, but in others it is not, for some constitutions function on different metabolic patterns. Increasing exercise only hastens the depletion, it does not produce renewal.

Occasionally—better say rarely—these pastors, by the careful conservation of what energy they do have, by concentrating on the things they do best, and by sheer dint of will power, develop and serve large churches. But they spend their lives forcing themselves to their duties. In most cases such energy-starved pastors are compelled to fulfill their calling in small churches. Some major on their studies and become useful writers. In any case, these pastors who stick with it in spite of weariness, even pain, are worthy of highest admiration and commendation. Opprobrium should never be heaped on them, even by innuendo, for not turning their little world upside down.

Resourcefulness

Successful pastors can at times utilize plans and aids from their church headquarters; but more often they devise their own. They are able to use to the full the resources they have. These are days when to succeed the pastor must be creative and innovative. He must be innovative in finding the right ways and times to be with his people, to attract community attention, to promote revival, to improve organizational and office systems, to enlist and train workers, to improve discipling and teaching methods. The resourceful pastor will find ways to meet these demands.

Tough-mindedness

A successful pastor has a high level of frustration tolerance. His poise is maintained under intense pressure. Furthermore, he exhibits a better-than-average capacity for detail. This is well, for more than many understand a pastor's capacity for detail may prove to be the quality which sets the ceiling of his opportunities. He may not *govern* every detail; but neither does he miss them. But a tough-minded pastor's capacity for detail is perfected by his capacity for complexity. For in the pastorate there are many different kinds of operations which must be understood and grasped. No one has more irons in the fire. This goes with the territory.

A further facet of tough-mindedness is a high degree of objectivity. A church leader observed once about a clergyman who had held several important positions, only to end them in a storm, "He has excellent judgment except when he becomes personally involved." He could not maintain his objectivity. A successful pastor learns to avoid becoming emotionally subjective, and to be able to perceive the best thing for the church in complete detachment from the preferred thing for himself. He seeks to be objective with himself, his friends, and his critics.

This involves the ability to see the whole as well as the parts and to maintain perspective. As an artist backs off from his painting and studies it thoughtfully as a whole, so must a pastor frequently disentangle himself from petty details that loom large, and realign and rebalance his view. Thus he can avoid the myopia which results in missing the forest for the trees. He does not permit his capacity for detail to become a pit in which he buries himself.

Maintaining perspective will prompt us to practice the maxims of John R. Mott, the great missionary statesman: "In a life that is lived economically, the major issue must always receive priority"; and "We must act at the point of maximum strategy; life is too short to do anything else." These principles will enable us to stay out of the trap of perfectionism that says, "If it is worth doing, it is worth doing well." True, if not taken too seriously. Everything in the ministry is worth doing, but not everything can be done so well as we would like, if the primary things are going to be done well. Even good things must be graded by a sliding scale of priority. A famous painter of sunsets was coaching a student who was absorbed in getting just right the detail of the shingles on the barn in the foreground while the beautiful sunset in the background was gradually fading. In disgust the master said, "You are going to have to make up your mind whether you are going to be a great painter of shingles or a great painter of sunsets."

Public ability

A successful pastor does not embarrass his people by bungling. He is capable. He compares favorably in the pulpit with the speakers his people have already heard on radio or TV before coming to church. He conducts a funeral or a wedding with competence and finesse. In a secular community situation, when asked to emcee, give an invocation, introduce a speaker, or express an opinion, he is adept in saying the right things and doing it the right way. He is neither combative nor fawning, but straightforward, poised, courteous, and helpful. (More about this in chapter 6.)

This public proficiency includes superior skill with words. The successful pastor communicates well. He is constantly alert to possible breakdowns in communication, which can be the monkey wrench in otherwise good churches. His ideas are clearly and persuasively expressed, with the result that his associates are not left guessing. Yet he does not drown his ideas with floods of verbiage. He does not talk an idea to death.

Nowhere is the ability to articulate well more vital than in the pulpit. This involves many related skills, but at least one is the ability to use words correctly. Just as the surgeon must know which instrument to use, so must a preacher know which word to use. Failure here hangs around the pastor's neck the albatross of apparent illiteracy. He may not be illiterate, but carelessness in the use of words will result in his being so tagged. While the best of preachers may have an occasional slip of the tongue, it had better be occasional rather than habitual.

QUALITIES OF PERSONAL CHARACTER

Discipline

When we speak of highly successful pastors, we mean pastors whose success is not just a splashy spurt but a steady and growing reality over many years. But only a disciplined person will achieve this. Undisciplined pastors—undisciplined in appetites and in time management—will become mentally and morally flabby, and will have diminishing returns until the returns disappear altogether.

The disciplined man or woman learns to control his moods, his desires, his tongue, and his time. He learns to say no to himself, and he learns to do what he knows he should be doing when he knows he should be doing it. Charles Lindbergh's advice to his sons is sound: "Do the toughest things first." And author James Newton observes that that was "a rule [Lindbergh] always applied to himself."[2]

The moral pressures on a pastor are enormous. Only a deep devotional life and disciplined living on every front will put sufficient iron in his moral fiber to protect him. The Holy Spirit is his enabling power, but the Spirit must be obeyed in daily disciplines, not grieved; otherwise in the moment of temptation he will be a modern Samson, shorn of his power, unaware that the Lord has "left him" (Judg. 16:20).

Sincerity

Insincerity cannot long be hid. The moment people begin to sense it, they inwardly withdraw. A sincere man or woman means what he/she says, both in the pulpit and out. A young man who was a skillful debater in college prided himself on his ability to debate either side of a question with equal persuasiveness. But in his first pastorate his wife kept asking, "Did you mean what you said in your sermon? Were you really sincere?" Her insistent probing led to his deep heart-searching and, as a result, his entire sanctification. The secret falseness was cleansed.

Sincerity makes one transparent. Nothing is mere window dressing, grandstanding, or cunning. There are no hidden agendas or ultimate motives. The sincere person feels what he says he feels and believes what he says he believes. His warm friendliness is not a practiced art camouflaging a cold heart, but the natural expression of the real person. The sincere man is bona fide in his piety, in his love for people, and in his desire to serve. Sincerity is never seasonal or opportunistic. It is not an occasional happening. It is a quality of the soul which defines the person. To be sincere at all is to be sincere all the time, in all places, and about everything. People will respect a pastor whose sincerity is unquestioned, and they will be more inclined to follow him.

Optimism

A highly successful pastor exudes faith and reassurance. He is not a pessimist. His approach is positive, inspiring, and uplifting rather than negative and depressing. He is this way in the office, in his home, in business meetings, and in the pulpit. Not that he carries no crushing burdens, or that his sermons have no stern prophetic note in them. But even in preaching against sin he lifts up Christ as the answer. He scatters encouragement, affirmation, and hope rather than gloom and despair.

Care

Even though the word is worn thin by overuse, *care* still denotes a universal quality of outstandingly successful pastors. They are "people persons." While they may also be goal-oriented, their drive to reach specific objectives is not at the expense of the personal touch. They like people. They are at home with people and people are at ease with them. Their true concern shows in everything they do. Children are drawn to them, as they were to Jesus. It is easy to confide in these pastors. But it is possible to be a strong preacher and a fairly good administrator without this quality of personal warmth and compassion.

Care is much deeper than charisma. Some preachers have affable and gifted personalities whose caring is only skin-deep. Therefore, they have to advertise themselves as caring. Real caring needs no trumpets sounding before it. It is obvious. It is the kind that carries people on one's mind. It remembers Mrs. Brown's rheumatism and Joe's unemployment; Mary's broken love affair; Molly and Fred's worry over their son in the military. These pastors can say with Paul, "I have you in my heart" (Phil. 1:7).

Magnetism

While the quality of caring is more vital than charisma, charisma is not to be deprecated as unimportant. Most successful pastors have that mysterious, undefinable magnetic appeal which draws people to them. It may include physical attractiveness, but not necessarily. The apostle Paul was not physically attractive; nevertheless he had a powerful personality. Without contriving to get attention, some persons unconsciously draw it. Their very presence is a focal point in any gathering. One either has this "presence" or he does not. If he does not, trying to achieve it by gimmicks of flashy dress or smart talk will repel rather than attract.

The Spirit-filled man or woman will worry very little over this quality of personal magnetism, but will yield to the Spirit's operation through him or her. The Holy Spirit is able to create a holy magnetism in a pastor who does not have it naturally. And like the new wine at Cana, this is better (John 2:10).

Consistency

"They are very stable," writes Laura Ost of the top corporate executives in America.[3] That's the way they got to the top. Likewise, a successful pastor carries through. He avoids frequent flip-flops and sudden changes of direction. He knows where he is going and keeps a steady hand on the wheel. The stands he takes today will be the stands he takes tomorrow. His people learn they can count on this. This makes for stability and a feeling of security.

Not that he is rigidly hidebound and inflexible or impervious to persuasion. He will change when it is time to change. If one plan does not work, he will try another. But he is not hopping from one idea to another before any of them has had a fair chance. Some pastors keep their people dizzy by their changeable, impulsive, and unpredictable operating style.

Resilience

Successful pastors recover their equilibrium quickly. They bounce back. They roll with the punches. With Paul they can testify to being "afflicted in every way, but not crushed; perplexed but not despairing; struck down [by bad votes?] but not destroyed" (2 Cor. 4:8–9, NASB). Or, as J. B. Phillips puts it, "we may be knocked down but we are never knocked out."

These pastors are like Paul at Lystra. There they "stoned Paul and dragged him outside the city, thinking he was dead. But after the disciples had gathered around him, he got up and went back into the city" (Acts 14:19–20). Perhaps this was sheer miracle. But the resilience of Philip the evangelist was sheer grace. After the great crowds and excitement in Samaria he found himself on a desert road being directed to one man. From the city to the desert! He didn't whine in self-pity but ran to obey when the Spirit said, "Go to that chariot and stay near it" (Acts 8:29). Resilient persons can handle both deflation and inflation, both criticism and praise, both bad votes and good votes. They don't roll over dead when reverses come; they look around for a new approach. Rather than capsizing they tack into contrary winds.

Wisdom

This quality belongs both to the category of "professional proficiency" and to the category of "personal character." It is the merging and fulfillment of both.

The first element of wisdom is common sense. The successful pastor knows where the borderline is between effective innovation and foolish stunts. He is courageous, sometimes daring, but never loses his head. He refuses to be pushed into harebrained schemes in the name of faith. He has a sense of propriety. He is aware of the eternal fitness of things. Some men so disregard protocol and convention that the public is repelled, and their churches and their religion become laughingstocks. They become notorious rather than respectably well known.

But wisdom is more than common sense. It is uncommon insight. It is the ability to sort primary ends from secondary and then to match means to ends. It is the understanding which senses moods and needs, and the sagacity to shape administrative policies to these moods and needs. It is the ability to draw together the disparate opinions and temperaments into a common phalanx of march.

Wisdom is a sense of timing and strategy. It is not to be confused with the cleverness which merely outwits the opposition. That borders too closely to the wisdom of "envying and strife" which is not "from heaven but is earthly, unspiritual, of the devil" (James 3:14–15). The true wisdom begins with love, proceeds with understanding, and ends with God-honoring solutions. It is marked by patience. It is the child of knowledge and faith. It is wise enough to be humble, and humility is wise enough to pray. Through prayer it gains insight and knows what to do and the right way to do it.

Wisdom is the good sense not to allow oneself to be stampeded and monopolized by one's obsessions. Pastors are human, and like everyone else occasionally get bees in their bonnet. One becomes obsessed with the need for a bus ministry, another becomes obsessed with two Sunday morning services, another obsessed with the need for enlarged staff, another obsessed with an obstruction in church affairs which seems to demand immediate removal. These obsessions can become so preoccupying that attention is distracted from everything else. Nothing else gets done until the pastor is able to work out his obsession. He needs the wisdom to refuse to allow his obsessions to distort his daily schedule and get out of proportion to the whole. He can learn to make haste slowly, and achieve the desired ends without sinking the ship.

Integrity

This is the character quality which crowns all the others. Without it one's showy success will sooner or later turn sour. The pastor's vaunted kingdom will collapse around him. A man with integrity is like Barnabas—"a good man" (Acts 11:24). Such a person is a safe risk in any home. He is a man of his word. Money is safe in his hands.

Integrity will not compromise principle for personal advantage. It will not sell out for votes. It scorns checking the direction of the wind to see which causes are safe. One pastor vigorously and boldly championed the "in" concerns—for a while wife abuse, then child abuse, then something else. But he never touched abortion. Though he was personally opposed to it, he left the issue alone: it was too "hot." *This is the expediency of the politician, not the prophet.* To let public opinion dictate our crusades casts a very long shadow over both one's sincerity and one's integrity.

Integrity is unflinching in its loyalty to commitments and obligations, whether marriage vows, church vows, or ordination vows. At this point there is no more subtle test of a pastor's integrity than the contemporary push for church growth. I say this with trepidation because these days raising one tiny question about church growth is like knocking motherhood. We are all for church growth as a matter of course; in fact, many of us need to be far more enthusiastic about it than we are. But church growth with integrity? Is this important? A little fudging here and there, a little discreet silence, a little overlooking of doctrinal distinctions can promote a show of growth more rapidly. In the end the pastor's soul will be corroded, and the Holy Spirit will be grieved. "Success" at the expense of integrity is success at too high a price.

These are the primary qualities of character and mind which characterize strong pastors. While there may be built-in limitations of energy and endowment in some cases, most of these qualities can be acquired. Intentional self-improvement can turn a pastor threatened with mediocrity, even failure, into the Lord's "mighty man of valor"—which, being translated, means an outstandingly successful pastor.

3

FOUNDATIONS FOR SUCCESS

Both Jesus and Paul stressed the importance of foundations. Only obedience to his words, Jesus said (Matt. 7:24–29), would provide a solid foundation for life and destiny. Paul's emphasis was on making sure that Christ Himself is the foundation for our Christian work (1 Cor. 3:11). He meant more than an easy verbal claim. The whole doctrine of Christ must undergird and locate everything we do: our preaching, administration, leadership—our total methodology. This is to say that our entire ministry must be controlled and shaped by everything Christ is and means—His deity, His saviorhood, His headship of the church, His ministry through the Spirit, His principles of operation.

For the pastor the desire to build on Christ must be confirmed by certain supportive conditions. In a sense these supportive conditions are elementary to the foundation itself.

A VALID CALL

What the Epistle to the Hebrews says about the priesthood can equally be said about the Christian ministry: "No one takes this honor upon himself; he must be

called by God" (Heb. 5:4). But unfortunately some good
men—even sanctified men—are self-called. Their very
sincerity and zeal have misled them. All soundly converted persons who are of an intense nature, and doubly
so when filled with the Spirit, have a passion for souls.
They are consumed by a fervent desire to serve God. They
yearn to win the world. It is natural, and has happened a
thousand times, for this inner fire to be mistaken for a call
to preach.

But once in the pastorate they are a round peg in a
square hole. Nothing works. They pray and scramble,
change locations, try this and that, but still their ministry
is flat. They can't preach. They have no "presence" in the
pulpit. In administration they flounder. The blunt truth is
they have missed their calling. Yet they are good men,
and would make excellent laymen. In spite of wounded
pride and acute embarrassment, their wisest course is to
admit their error and quietly stand aside and boost and
pray while someone else does the job.

Closely akin to the tragedy of the mistaken call is the
debacle of being, even if truly called to the ministry, in the
wrong place. Both the calling and the deployment belong
to God. Many a person has elbowed his way into a church
for which he was not suited. Both the church and the man
suffer.

A call of God to the ministry does not mean that
success is possible everywhere. Some churches and men
are plain mismatches, not made in heaven. What God has
joined together let not man put asunder, but what *man*
has "joined" through the finagling of the flesh let God
mercifully put asunder, and the sooner the better.

The spiritual and intellectual giant J. Glenn Gould
was given as his first pastorate a strong city church. He
soon knew he was in over his head. At the end of the year
he said to the district superintendent, "I'm not ready for
this yet. Give me the smallest and toughest church on the

district." That's what he got and that was the place of his first success. His intelligent self-appraisal and courageous action were portents of his future stature.

Yet it is possible for some discouraged preacher reading these lines to misapply them to himself. He is having a rough time and the idea that he has made a mistake in accepting this church may seem to offer a logical way out. If he positively knows he disobeyed God in coming, he had better pray for forgiveness and ask God to release him. Then wait for God's method. If he got ahead of the Lord in coming, don't let him compound his error by getting ahead of the Lord in leaving. There is a right and wrong way. The right way begins with one's ecclesiastical superior and following his counsel. To sneak out in the middle of the night (as has happened) will jeopardize one's entire future.

But discouraging setbacks may not in themselves be evidences of being out of divine order. Let the pastor review the providences and impressions which led him to this charge. If, as he prays and remembers, the sense of call is renewed, let him hold steady. To kick the traces now will be to miss a great personal victory and perhaps miss out on a pastoral breakthrough just around the corner.

Here therefore we have a dual pillar in one's foundation for success—the certainty of a divine call to the ministry, and the equal certainty that I am right now where God wants me to be.

THE PASTOR'S EQUIPMENT

Every God-called prospective pastor has potential abilities which make success possible. Failure will be his fault, not God's. But the potential powers must be brought out and developed to a level of effectiveness. This is a lifelong process. At some point along the line of this development it is reasonable to launch the person in a pastorate. But the development, requiring discipline and rigorous application, must go on, or the pastor will hang around the level of mediocrity, teetering on the edge of staying in the ministry or falling out.

A good mind

Illiteracy can be remedied by education, clumsiness by culture, but not much can be done about native dullness. Amazingly enough, in the past even medical doctors have practiced in spite of a low IQ. Certainly some preachers have crashed the gates in spite of mental deficiencies. After the antics of one such, the district superintendent commented to me, "That dear brother has more religion and less sense than anyone I know." Good religion does not necessarily expand gray matter. Good judgment is born of intelligence as well as good intentions.

Broad knowledge

It is impossible for a pastor to know too much. No field of knowledge in which he has acquired expertise need be wasted; all can be turned to good account. The possible danger in such wide knowledge might be the situation of the preacher who allows his expertise to siphon off time and energy which should be devoted to the church. One of the most brilliant and talented young preachers I ever knew nevertheless failed because he was too expert in his hobbies. He puttered in many things and failed to focus on his main job.

In another case a pastor brought into the ministry unusual skills both as a carpenter and as an auto mechanic. In unwise kindheartedness he came to the rescue of his church members in their handyman and automotive needs to the extent that his study was neglected. The result was a negative vote in three successive pastorates—voted out by the very people who called on him to fix their cars or mend their roofs! This is not what I mean by saying that all kinds of knowledge can be assimilated into the pastoral and preaching ministry. While a pastor who is a good mechanic is not smart to be forever tinkering with cars, he is wise to use his knowledge as illustrations for his sermons or as a point of contact in pastoral calling.

A pastor should know theology. In fact he should have a good theological foundation before he presumes to pastor a church. If he is incapable of acquiring this knowledge or too lazy to do so, please let him continue digging ditches or selling real estate. How can a man preach the gospel if he doesn't understand it? And let no pastor betray his own ignorance by despising theology and making derogatory wisecracks about theologians. At bottom every important question is a theological one. Every person who thinks enough to ask the big questions and tries to answer them is theologizing—even if he professes to be an atheist. So a pastor cannot escape being a theologian any more than a physician can escape being a medical man. If it is a crime for a doctor to trifle with the bodies of his patients by willful ignorance, it is a double crime for preachers to presume to deal with judgment-bound souls, when "they do not know what they are talking about" (1 Tim. 1:7).

Furthermore, a pastor who would hope to succeed needs some reasonable understanding of people. He should be a lifelong student of human nature, first from the Bible, second from life, and third from the study of psychology and related disciplines.

As far as possible, he should know science, pedagogy, history, and literature. He should acquire a mastery of his own language so that he will not advertise himself as illiterate every time he opens his mouth, but most of all so that he can better convey the magnificent truths with which he is entrusted. The oratorios of Handel deserve something better than a tin horn or a broken fiddle.

The pastor should have some competency in business, economics, sociology, law, and political science. These fields should not consume the lion's share of his time or attention. But he should be sufficiently informed that he can administrate his church and serve his community without embarrassment; and perhaps even speak to one of the local civic clubs.

"The long run"

The acquisition of knowledge and related skills we call education. Most denominations require a prescribed level of preparation before they will entrust a man or woman with ordination. Ideally, this should be obtained via liberal arts college and seminary. However, a called person may in some groups become ordained by the route of a home-study course or a Bible college. Other things being equal, the chances of success, *over the long haul,* are greater if the slower, longer route of training is chosen. If nothing else, the greater discipline, effort, and sacrifice required augurs well for the increased stature needed for the job. J. B. Chapman's little conversation with his wife is well known. After serving fruitfully as a self-taught evangelist for several years and with a wife and several children, he said, "Do you believe that if I took time out to attend college for four years I would accomplish more for God in the long run?" She said, "Yes." And so they did because he added, "It's the long run we are on." Succeeding in the pastorate is hard enough at best without jeopardizing our chances in advance by skimpy and shallow preparation.

Overcoming odds

However, there is another side to this coin. Seminary is not a surety of success nor the home-study course of failure. Many have succeeded with only the home-study course, while scores of bright seminary graduates have miserably fizzled. In tipping the scales three factors far outweigh formal education: character, prayer life, and study habits. If the husband and wife are made of the right stuff and can demonstrate courage, persistence, patience, a right spirit, and a true service motive, and if they truly love God and people, they will have an unerasable impact for God in spite of limited education. Then if the pastor is a man of prayer, God can help him make maximum use of what resources he has and in the process add to them.

The third factor is a habit of lifelong study. The pastor who continues to study will keep growing even into his golden years; whereas no matter how many degrees a man earns in the beginning of his ministry, if he relies on that intellectual capital he will die "at the top." Intellectually stagnating, he will become both bored and boring and an easy prey to some diverting enticement by the time he reaches middle age.

A classic example of making optimum use of limited education is the case of the preacher we shall call Jones. With only a three-year Bible institute education beyond high school, he felt inferior on his district. Finally, after several years, it suddenly dawned on him that really his fellow pastors and his parishioners were not half so concerned with his educational pedigree as they were with his productivity. Emancipated, he threw himself into the work with new commitment and enthusiasm. He wrote out his sermons. He read and studied. He worked hard. He became a powerful preacher, a great leader, a skilled administrator—reaching before retirement the district superintendency and membership on the general administrative body of his denomination. Later when a new dean was to be installed at his denominational seminary, guess who was asked to do it. The moral? Limited education may be a disadvantage but not fatally so. It is the man that counts. A thirst for knowledge, a love of books, a teachable spirit, a passion for improvement, a servant's mind-set, a willingness to work, and a disciplined lifestyle will overcome almost any initial educational handicap.

THE DIVINE DYNAMIC

To say that a preacher who is to succeed must be in a good state of grace is to display an admirable perception of the obvious. But before we start taking too much for granted, we should point out two things.

First, it is possible to have a grand show of success without any grace at all. Able and ambitious men who enjoy the ministry as a vocation can in their own energies be effective speakers, affable friends, dynamic leaders, and skilled administrators. They can fill churches. In another country a young minister confided to a friend, "I have two ambitions—to become the head of my denomination and to become the country's top Mason." He reached both goals. There was not a bit of God anywhere along the line. We need to see clearly that splashy statistics are no evidence of spiritual genuineness. Conversely, limited statistics may accompany deep spirituality.

The second observation is more depressing, because closer home. It is possible to be able to pronounce all the shibboleths and still be working in the energy of the flesh. Our doctrine may be correct, and we may be born again yet still be carnally motivated. We may give all the right answers to the examining boards yet be void of the evidence of divine power in our ministry.

The bottom line is that the success which will stand when the world is on fire, which is "gold, silver, precious stones" instead of "wood, hay, stubble" (1 Cor. 3:12, KJV), is impossible without the anointing of the Holy Spirit. This means divine power flowing through a pure heart and resting upon a holy life.

"I am convinced," writes Samuel Shoemaker, "that much of our preaching about Christ consists of well-meant words that lack the authentication which would bring them to life; and that authentication can come only as we ourselves live more profoundly and more consistently in the Spirit."[1]

In commenting on "Coming Into the Stream of the Spirit," he says, "The trouble with a lot of us is that we have never been broken." Later he observes, "There is a death to self in coming into the stream of the Spirit."[2]

A young pastor who was doing so-so was shocked by his father-in-law who said to him, "You don't have much anointing on your preaching, do you?" He was hurt at first, even tempted to be offended. But he began to pray. One Saturday morning he stayed on his knees at the church altar until he knew he was "dead" and the Holy Spirit had indeed taken possession. Soon things began to happen in his church. He launched no new programs. He did not double his calling. He hired no new staff members. He made no sweeping changes in his organization. But God began to work. Sinners began to be converted; believers began to seek for heart holiness— and find it. When I was there in a revival I found a rare phenomenon: laymen instructing seekers for holiness and praying them through as skillfully as any preacher. It all began when the young pastor obtained the divine anointing upon his ministry.

But it cannot be said too often: The anointing will

never rest upon a man's ministry unless the blessing of God is on the man. Empowerment presupposes cleansing. Meeting God at an altar means facing up to sin. If we are careless in our morals, shabby in our ethics, quarrelsome at home, petty and pouty with people, we will have no power from God. No purity, no power. This is simply the way God's kingdom operates.

We are not to conclude that because the divine dimension is so basic the human factors no longer matter. The young pastor was already a good preacher. He was already a good pastor. He was already an exemplary family man. He already had a well-organized church. The machinery was in place; it needed only the power of God upon it at a stepped-up level in order for the machinery to become God's instrument for doing what God so much wanted to do. So we keep God and man together as God intends. Man's abilities are naught without the energizing of the Spirit. But the Spirit works through the human and may be either hindered or helped by the degree of man's submission and cooperation.

In a recent commencement address at the Nazarene Theological Seminary, David L. McKenna, president of Asbury Theological Seminary, said:

> Lloyd John Ogilvie tells the story in his latest book, *The Other Jesus*, of his trip as a young clergyman to New College in Edinburgh, Scotland. He confesses that his relationship to Christ at that time was "bordered north, south, east, and west by Lloyd." He busied himself doing the work of Christ without ever facing up to his deep need for the transforming power of Christ's cross. One day in a class taught by Thomas Torrance, he used carefully stated questions to avoid the truth of his professor's teaching. Torrance saw his need and challenged, "Mr. Ogilvie, you can't sneak around Golgotha. You must die." While Torrance explained what it meant to die to self, to pride, and to his own plans, priorities, and personality, Lloyd listened in shocked silence. Lloyd gave his total self to Christ, and with that act, Christ's death became not only real but his only hope.

Then McKenna added, "I call you this day, along with myself to the radical self-death at the Cross of Jesus Christ by which the infilling of His Holy Spirit can make us Christians with passion, ministering to the needs of those who are hurting in our world of self-interest."[3]

4

THE PASTOR'S
PERSONAL LIFE

According to the Bible a pastor must be "above reproach" (1 Tim. 3:2). This blamelessness is a must in at least three basic areas: personal character, family life, and business relations.

THE CHARACTER FACTOR

There will be no divine dynamic in one's ministry unless one's baptism with the Spirit is validated by strong moral character. In the secular world the claim is often made that one's private life away from the job is none of the public's concern. This claim is being blatantly voiced by school teachers, elected officials, and many others in the public eye. But such a position taken by a preacher is the crowning imbecility. A young pastor of my acquaintance flung such defiance at his concerned church leaders when, after his wife left him, he started shining around his young secretary. Only eternity will reveal the irreversible damage done before the church managed to get him out. Such an attitude reflects an immature philosophy of life, a hireling's view of the ministry, and an impudence toward God.

In June 1988, Chuck Colson addressed some 200

Prison Fellowship leaders in their annual planning meeting. After reviewing God's blessings and detailing the open doors before them, he asked, "How are we going to accomplish these tasks?" Then immediately he countered: "But that is the wrong question to ask. The important question is, What kind of people are we going to be?" He answered by discussing four qualities of *being* which they must possess, the first of which was *holiness*.[1] Stephen F. Olford makes the same point: "God is far more concerned with what we are than what we do. If what we are doesn't satisfy his holy demands, then what we do is virtually worthless."[2]

While taking a walk one day, I admired the neatly kept yard of a house on the corner. But as I turned the corner and walked down the side of the house I caught a glimpse, through a gate slightly ajar, of the unkempt backyard. Weeds, piles of trash, and uncut grass were supposedly hidden behind the high fence. The contrast between what was displayed to the public and what was hidden was shocking. Sometimes there is an unsuspected backyard in a pastor's life. But sooner or later some gate will be left open and the truth will be discovered. When that happens that pastor's influence is at a dead end. And the bigger the show on Sunday morning the bigger will be the nausea in the stomachs of his people. For the sake of his soul, he needs to confess, clean up, ask forgiveness— then get out. For even if he recovers himself spiritually, it is doubtful that the tarnish to his image in the church and community can ever be quite removed.

"A good name is more desirable than great riches," the Preacher says (Prov. 22:1). But the good name will not outlast its basis in good character. A man or woman of character is a person not only of sterling integrity but of courage, discipline, perseverance, and rock-ribbed stability. Such a pastor may wince but will not whine. He or she is a tower of strength on whom a whole congregation will come to depend.

THE PASTOR'S FAMILY LIFE

Sometimes a pastor's family is the millstone around his neck. A gossipy, garrulous, bossy wife can render her husband's talents unmarketable. As for the children, one wonders how many empty parsonages there would suddenly be if 1 Timothy 3:4 were strictly enforced: "He must manage his own family well and see that his children obey him with proper respect."

However, an even more insurmountable barrier to success is for that millstone around the pastor's neck to be not his wife or his children but his own relationship with them. He, of all men, can rightfully be expected to model the husband and father described in Ephesians: "Husbands, love your wives," and "Fathers, do not exasperate your children; instead, bring them up in the training and instruction of the Lord" (5:25; 6:4). A gushy public show of love will not do; nor will public admonitions. The real home life, including both husband-wife and parent-child relations, should be solid and exemplary.

His right arm

Such a home is a pastor's most effective arm of ministry. For such a home cannot be hid; indeed it should not be. People yearn to see with their own eyes what a normal Christian home is like. Visiting children and teenagers imbibe indelible impressions which will fashion their own dreams and ideals and reinforce their faith. But if instead of love they find bickering, yelling, and general disorder, they will be disillusioned and wounded, and perhaps lost both to Christ and the church.

The parsonage family privacy should be guarded up to a reasonable point, but not to an extreme isolation as if the public were poison. The home should be the pastor's haven, true. Yet somewhere in here must be remembered the injunction, "given to hospitality" (1 Tim. 3:2, KJV). But hospitality is a family affair; the pastor cannot be hospitable by himself. Furthermore, hospitality is an atmosphere, a spirit, which makes guests feel wanted and cherished.

The health of the wife and ages of the children are factors which will bear on how much the home is to be accessible to outsiders. But the truth is that many solid Christians today trace their spiritual strength in great measure to the happy hours in the parsonage as teens or to the meals shared and loving fellowship offered, with prayers and tears mingled. The pastor's home life—how he lives in it and what he does with it—simply cannot be dismembered from his total ministry. It is a facet of that ministry, for good or ill.

It will bear repeating that the pastor has no better church building tool than his own home. In an early pastorate we were told, when we moved into the parsonage, that three of the newer couples (not yet members) had decided to use the pastoral change as the opportunity to visit other churches. Within two weeks we had all three couples, separately, into the parsonage for a hot dinner. They were enthralled. They had never before been invited guests at a parsonage meal. We cemented all three couples to us and to the church. There was no more talk of going elsewhere. Instead, in due course they joined and became solid pillars.

Total involvement

The happiest parsonages and the most useful parsonage families are where there is total involvement in the work of the church. Everyone, yes, including the children, see themselves as part of the team. They share the enthusiasms, the planning, the victories, and to some extent, even the burdens and sorrows. To suppose that children should be shielded from the realities of their father's work is a great mistake. It misjudges their capacity for caring, and it deprives them of the greatest arena for growth known by any family in the congregation. Involved children are less apt to grow up resenting their role as PKs. They learn to think of others; they understand why Dad is gone some evenings; they develop at an early age a sense of responsibility; their emotional roots become profoundly grounded and entwined with the church and all it stands for. Out of such a parsonage will come faithful laymen, preachers, and missionaries.

Whether or not children of pastors grow up a part of the team or alien to it depends largely on the attitude of the parents. If the parents are resentful, full of self-pity (or misguided pity for the children), the mood will be contagious. Children will absorb the atmosphere by osmosis. But this is a spiritual problem. If the parents will surrender totally, not to the church but to God, and accept His yoke gladly with every fiber of their being, and glory in their role as ambassadors and shepherds, their high sense of privilege will buoy everything they do, and their sheer joy will be transmitted to the children.[3]

Not only is the atmosphere of the parsonage a spiritual matter but it is philosophical as well. If husband and wife have imbibed the modern notion that their private personhood and individuality are more important than teamwork, that the wife should go her way, the children theirs, and the pastor his, the likelihood that the children will grow up with any sense of responsibility toward the church will be slight if not nil. And such fragmented parsonage families are certainly not happier; neither will their members be healthier—in the long run—for having been shielded from the pressures of the ministry.

The argument that since there is only one salary, there should be only one worker, is a carnal argument which knows nothing about consecration, divine love, or the joy of the Spirit. A sanctified pastor's wife is in it with her husband all the way, praying with him, bearing him up, sharing his burdens, helping in whatever way she can, and doing it gladly for Jesus' sake. The question of pay never enters her head. A separate career is not the way to preserve personal identity or mental health. The best assurance for these blessings is the inner peace of knowing we are pleasing God.

The working wife

The primordial working wife is the homemaker. Her job is the most challenging career possible, and, other things being equal, her faithfulness in this role is the best way by far to support her husband. No amount of money she might earn elsewhere could possibly compensate for the handicap her absence from the parsonage introduces into their total ministry. Doubly ludicrous is it when her outside job ties him down to part-time baby-sitting—thus crippling his ministry rather than aiding it.

But having said this it must be added that in some extreme situations it may be justified for a pastor's wife to work outside the home. This is especially likely to be the case in church-planting enterprises. If a wife, who would rather stay at home, courageously and unselfishly expends herself in order to release her husband for church work, and if this is actually the result, then she merits our admiration and approbation—certainly not brickbats.

The pastor's conduct

While much depends on the wife, the achievement of a happy parsonage is even more dependent on the pastor. He must avoid three common mistakes:

1. *Churlishness.* If he is selfish and unreasonable, if he is cross with his wife and impatient with the children, if he loses his temper, he spoils everything. He had better pull the blinds and lock the doors and keep his church members outside. But that is not holiness. Let such a pastor humble himself before God until he is changed totally, in reactions, in spirit, in voice timbre, in understanding. The atmosphere of the home will rise no higher than the atmosphere which the father brings with him when he enters the door. Let him park his grumpiness outside. Better yet, get it out of his heart.

One pastor reared five children—all of them now active in the church. The oldest child told me that they looked back remembering their father's gentleness toward their mother—a diminutive, not strong, but courageous woman. When he would come home from his study at the church or after a day of calling their father would say to her, "Would you like for me to help you finish getting the dinner on?" And her answer would be, "Yes, please do."

In another case a preacher's wife told me that before she was married she did not believe in the possibility of full sanctification. Then she said, "But I do now; I have lived with a sanctified man for twenty years." When the wife believes it, the children will too; and beyond that the church people will believe it.

2. *A driving spirit.* It is possible for even a sanctified pastor unwittingly to become uptight. The first thing he knows he is doing the Lord's work not in the power of the Spirit but in the energy of the flesh. He becomes inwardly driven. But such a spirit never stops with him. The aggressive, pushy, often demanding spirit is felt by his people, sometimes transmitted to them; but worse yet, he takes it home with him. He becomes unreasonable in his demands with the children, expecting a perfection from them beyond their capability. And he multiplies his expectations of his wife, imposing loads and duties and

activities beyond her strength. Laughter and play become casualties. Emotional wedges begin to divide and weaken. This happens not because the pastor is evil or means to be unkind, but because he has allowed himself to become obsessed with a driving spirit. He must stop, back off, relax, play and laugh again, apologize, renew his own spirit, and realign his perspective. After all, it is the Lord's work, not his.

An editor of a monthly pastor's journal received an anonymous letter from a harried parsonage wife. She narrated her predicament—four small boys, several jobs in the church, increasing weariness, all compounded by a driving husband who failed to understand her needs. When she tried to talk with him, he would explode, "Here I am, working like a slave to make this church go, and surely I should be able to expect you to carry your end of the load!" Anonymous or not, the letter was quietly traced and identified, and word was passed to the superintendent who could move in with his restraining hand before that well-meaning young pastor blew his home apart, and his ministry to boot.

3. *Neglect.* A lively discussion is abroad these days concerning the relative priority of the pastor's family in relation to the church. Having heard dire tales of neglect and its horrible consequences, some young pastors are so determined to put their family first that the church is shoved to the back burner. Family first is really very little different from "me" first—it is a composite "me." Everyone in the family may end up ingrown and protective of self but casual about the church. Is this really what the pastor wants?

No more useful laymen ever blessed a denomination than Rhoda and Gordon Olson, of Eugene, Oregon. As pressing as their business always was, church had priority. One of their two sons said, "When we were growing up there was never any question as to which came first, the church or our own interests. We knew the church would always be put first; we never expected anything else." It is temporizing and compromising which poisons children, not loving, consistent commitment. These two sons in their warm loyalty to the church and to Christ illustrate the principle. If it will work that way in a lay family, why not in the parsonage?

Faithful laymen are out at night a lot also, attending board meetings, committee meetings, a myriad of activities. Their wives too may wish their husbands could spend a quiet evening with them. But for that matter, so do the wives of doctors, policemen, firemen, insurance adjusters, sailors and soldiers, explorers. So the lonely pastor's wife should reflect long and hard about her many sister fellow-sufferers before she allows resentment to embitter her soul. For a woman to leave her preacher-husband, break up her home, and cripple his ministry, when she knows he is honestly seeking to build the kingdom only betrays a profound self-centeredness, and a backslidden heart.

Yet with all that, needless neglect is too common and should be avoided. While some demands such as emergency hospital calls are unavoidable, many activities are the creations more of zeal than wisdom. Pastors could often accomplish more at a slower pace. Frequent quiet, unhurried times with the children and other times just with the wife until emotions are nourished and renewed should be systematically planned and jealously guarded, within the limits of professional obligation.

Perhaps Don Wellman had it about right. When asked which should come first, the church or the family, he answered, "Neither. God should come first. If God does he will show us [what to do]. At times He will direct us to put the church first, while at other times He will prompt us to put the family first."

THE PASTOR AND MONEY

Not only do foundations for success include healthy family relationships, but irreproachable business activities. Carelessness around church finances or in handling personal credit accounts can result in suspicion and distrust, which ultimately will tarnish the glittering shine of one's hard work.

In the project of raising funds for the church in Jerusalem, Paul was doubly careful to protect himself from the slightest breath of scandal by appointing someone else to handle the money. And he explains why: "We want to avoid any criticism of the way we administer this liberal gift. For we are taking pains to do what is right, not only in the eyes of the Lord but also in the eyes of men" (2 Cor. 8:20–21).

The test of a pastor's ability to supervise church finances is his success in handling his own. Paul applies the question to the family, but if we add "finances" the point is made: "If anyone does not know how to manage his own family [finances], how can he take care of God's church?" (1 Tim. 3:5). Good question.

The pastor, for instance, who leaves unpaid bills when he changes churches, then pays no attention to the increasingly irate collection letters which follow him, is a disgrace to the ministry. The sooner he is found out and gotten out the better. He brings every other minister— indeed the Christian church, yes, Christ himself—into disrepute. He displays a fatal deficiency in both integrity and competence. Even if through unwise management debt has accrued, there are always ways to protect one's credit and the good name of the church. It is the silence which is inexcusable—in the meanwhile buying even more things and piling one's debts even higher. And it is to be feared that too often blaming the church for not paying enough is a copout for poor management. To allow money to crowd us out of the ministry is a sin against God. It reveals lack of dedication, faith, and discipline.

Some young couples are subconsciously infected with the materialism of the age. As a consequence they demand a higher standard of living than they have yet earned or the church can afford. When a man puts a price tag on his ministry, that moment he becomes a hireling. His whole attitude is totally foreign to the servanthood of Christ or the selfless love of an apostle Paul. Doubly odious is it to measure the value of education and degrees in terms of salary level such degrees should bring. Do young people struggle through school in order to have bigger churches and bigger salaries, or to prepare themselves better to serve the Lord? A mercenary approach to education degrades it and annuls its spiritual value. Such an attitude disqualifies one from a Spirit-empowered ministry.

One superintendent was trying to place a young couple about to graduate from seminary, but each church he offered prompted the complaint, "We can't live on what that church is offering." They had bought this and that, and had saddled themselves with substantial monthly obligations. Finally in disgust he said, "I think you two had better forget the whole thing. It looks to me as if you are more interested in your comforts than in the ministry." Contrast that couple with another who, when responding to a call to preach, let their fancy furniture go back, rearranged their affairs so they could take whatever opened, then went to the most unpromising church on the district, with meager salary—a faith-move which launched them upon a glorious adventure of thirty-five years of successful pastoral ministry.

Some situations call for a bi-vocational ministry. Especially is this expected to be the case when a couple accepts a church-planting mission. But the aim should be to make such an arrangement as temporary as possible. When not in the church-planters category but in an established church with a parsonage and a salary—no matter if small—the husband and wife can demonstrate both their mettle and their faith by saying to each other, "We are in this thing together, all the way, 'sink or swim, survive or perish!'" If God has called them and if they work hard and manage prudently, they will not perish. God thinks too much of His honor. They may not drive a luxury car but so what?

AN ADDENDUM TO WIVES

In a West Virginia parsonage, while I was at the church for a short revival meeting, I said to the pastor's wife, "Can you be happy in this house?" It was an old house, with marks of age and decrepitude in every room. With a radiant face she said quietly and simply: "I can be happy anywhere." I believed her. The relaxed, comfortable atmosphere in the home confirmed her words.

What was her secret—or perhaps *secrets?* I can guess the basic ones. First, she loved God and was consecrated to Him. Second, she loved her husband and believed in him. I suspect also that there was an emotionally satisfying relationship between them. But there was something else: her own decision. Some wives will never be happy in the ministry, no matter what the salary or how swank is the parsonage. They do not intend to be.

As one parsonage mother said to her teenagers, "We create our own moods." And wives create their own overall frame of mind by which they relate themselves to their husband's calling. It is a blend of divine grace and personal decision.

Of course if some preacher's wife testifies, "I began to be happy in the ministry when I put money, moves, and people on the altar, died out to my own way, and was truly sanctified," I will concur that this, after all, is the bottom line.

This much I do know. If a woman is going to succeed as a preacher's wife, her motivation must be deeper than love for her husband. Her inner drive must flow from something other than a human desire to see him succeed. Only an all-embracing and profound personal relationship with Jesus Christ, which transcends and sanctifies her love for her husband, will hold her steady during the lean years. If human love is all she has, she will be apt to become bitter and resentful when there are "no" votes, or when her husband is unfairly criticized, or when he doesn't get the ecclesiastical break she thinks he deserves. Conversely her strong grip on God may many times be the saving difference in the ability of her husband to hold steady, when battered and bruised. Husbands and wives should reinforce each other, not just professionally but spiritually and emotionally. Then they will share in the joys and rewards.

5

GETTING OFF TO A GOOD START

Long-range success in a pastorate depends greatly on what happens the first six months. Just as a young husband can reduce his chances for a happy marriage by his folly on his honeymoon, so a new pastor can do more damage in the early days than he can undo in years—and in some cases more than he can ever undo. One pastor (usually very successful) said about an especially difficult church where he had mired himself hopelessly and could be extricated only by a move, "If I had taken three years to do what I tried to do in six months, I would be there yet."

THAT FIRST PASTORATE

I had occasion to visit a former seminary student who had been in his first pastorate less than a year. In fatherly freedom I poured out advice about first pastorates. I said, "There should be no sharp corners turned; no throwing one's pastoral weight around. The first year at least should be a year of establishing human relations. Get acquainted with the people and let them get acquainted with you on an amiable, nonthreatening, nonadversarial basis. Avoid changes which could produce restlessness and uneasiness." He replied, "Oh! I wish you could have told me that when I first came! I have already violated those principles and I'm already in trouble." Indeed he was, and he could not stay beyond two years. It was true that he faced mountains of carnality and some obstreperous people. But that fact was all the more reason for deliberate caution. J. B. Chapman used to say, "Don't stir up a nest of snakes unless you are sure you can kill them."

The age factor

Certain principles apply especially to a young man in his first pastorate. For one thing most of the people are older, and in many cases wiser, than he. Some of them were paying the bills and fighting the devil before he was born. They are willing to give him the benefit of the doubt and follow his leadership—up to a point. They admire his vigor and enthusiasm. But they will not follow a young leader just getting started in the way they will follow an older, more experienced man. A man in his forties can get away with actions and words which a beginner cannot.

Confidence cannot be demanded, it must be earned. And that takes time. Firmly rooted respect cannot be deeply established over night, not even by a few brilliant sermons or by boundless displays of energy. But does not Paul say to Timothy, "Let no man despise thy youth"? He does indeed, but let us hope Timothy was wise enough to know that a rejection of leadership on the grounds of youth could not be prevented by a stentorian command in the pulpit or an announcement in the bulletin, but by Timothy and all subsequent "Timothys" setting an "example for the believers in speech, in life, in love, in faith and in purity" (1 Tim. 4:12).

It is true that in most denominations church law gives to a pastor basic prerogatives as a leader. He is ex officio head of the local governing body, the church schools, missionary and youth societies, the music department, and whatever committees may be established. Even the youthful man in his first pastorate is expected to assume this leadership, but let it be done quietly, flexibly, cautiously, and with sincere deference to persons already established in leadership positions. The structure which a pastor finds should usually be confirmed not torn apart the first six weeks. Let not the new pastor use all his power, any more than a teenage driver should push his foot clear to the floor. Legal prerogatives are like money in the bank: spend it all at once and you will be out on the street.

The difficulty of restraint

Such caution, so important during the first six months, is difficult for a man right out of school to exercise. For years he has been building up steam and finally he has a chance to prove his stuff. His imagination has been fed by books and professors and ballyhooed superchurch pastors and visiting lecturers until he is sincerely confident he knows exactly how to do the job. He has studied psychology and management and church administration; and of course he has studied church growth until the lingo flows easily from his lips and its principles almost pop out of his ears. He is like the young seminarian who, when he was being shown a beautiful new church plant, enthusiastically got behind the pulpit, flexed his arms, and exclaimed, "What couldn't I do with a set-up like this!"

Why then do so many of these fireballs fizzle? Why do so many fall flat on their faces the first year? Because they understand everything but human nature. The first principle of human nature in the average congregation is that *People don't like change.* As Lyle E. Schaller says, "All

of us are more comfortable with continuity than disconti-
nuity."[1] Young people sometimes crave the excitement of
change, but not the people who pay the bills and who
constitute the power structure. When the eager young
preacher introduces countless novelties in the worship
services and springs on the church undigested schemes
for exploding numerically and (worse yet) begins talking
about a building program almost before his books are
unpacked, he is only tying his own noose. The lovely,
patient older folk (who have seen all this before) will
watch in amused fascination, wondering what the young
pastor will pull next. At first they will wait tolerantly, but
then with growing restiveness and resistance. And when
he begins to feel the resistance he will begin to push and
drive all the harder. He will call for prayer (always a good
idea), preach on cooperation, preach against carnality
(which he thinks is the problem). But the more he
thrashes the more they resist, to his deepening frustration
and their growing irritation.

LATER PASTORATES, TOO

But the initial period of a new pastorate is just as
crucial for an older man as for a beginner. Burning rubber
is a poor way to start. He, even more than the young
man, will see what needs to be done, and will, because of
experience, feel that he can take the wheel firmly and
forthrightly. The sudden turns he takes and the changes
he makes may all be for the better, and he may seem to be
carrying the church with him. Furthermore, he may
ultimately succeed in establishing his style of leadership
in spite of early bumpy roads. But he also may be subtly
undermining himself, and planting time bombs of resentment which down the line will blow him right into his
next pastorate.

The need for stability

This is true for several reasons. People love their church, their fellow members, their way of doing things, their building. They have a vested interest in things as they are. They have deep feelings of affection and attachment to the status quo. For them this constitutes stability. Too many changes, too rapidly made, which affect their positions and the positions of their friends or traditional ways of doing things can be traumatic. Furthermore, they naturally resent a new whirlwind quick-change artist who in effect is casting reflection upon their previous operating style—in plain language, making both them and his predecessor look stupid. Of course those who didn't like his predecessor will sic him on. But others will not.

The mature saints will try to manifest a good spirit and cooperate with the program. But underneath a slight questioning begins to form in their minds. Does this pastor really know what he is doing? Is he a truly wise leader or merely on an ego trip? Or perhaps a sincere bungler? Then they will discover that others feel the same way. Gradually an undercurrent of restlessness will develop which could, down the line, become an unexpected ground swell of opposition.

The need for time

Therefore, it is as wise for the more experienced pastor as for the young man to spend the first year getting acquainted. Things are not always as they seem in those first six weeks which bloom with promise. People are not always what they appear to be. Some are better, others are a lot worse. It is easy in the early days to play into the hands of the wrong people.

While the peril may be the excessive drive and eagerness of the pastor to produce overnight miracles, the peril may equally be in certain members of the congregation who see the new pastor as their opportunity to push their pet project (or peeve), or maybe reestablish themselves in former positions of power. So they may try to stampede the pastor into precipitate action which later he will profoundly regret.

One woman got the ear of her new pastor with piously told accounts of the terrible tongue of another woman in the church. This went on for some time, until she managed to make him feel that any pastor was a coward who would not deal with this situation. So, wanting to appear brave and faithful, he took a male board member with him and called on the hapless woman. He proceeded to rebuke her soundly, much to her hurt and astonishment and much to the embarrassment of the board member who accompanied him and who knew the facts better. The pastor learned later that he had been used by a carnal woman who wanted to enforce her will. Furthermore, in that foolish burst of heroics he planted the seeds of his negative vote three years later. It is better not to be stampeded into trying to prove one's bravery!

SOME RIGHT THINGS TO DO

What, therefore, are some positive approaches to this need for getting off to a good start?

Take charge with sensitivity

Everyone stares at the new preacher when the moment comes for him to take charge of his first service. An invisible but enveloping cloud of goodwill hangs in the air. The expectant and excited congregation wish him well. They are predisposed to like him. They want him to be the man they have imagined him to be. They want him to succeed among them as their shepherd.

His nervousness may tip off a few fumblings, but they will not be held against him, especially if he can laugh at himself. It could be that capable lay leaders or staff members have planned this first service so that all he is expected to do is preach. Or, more likely, he will have planned the service himself and will be in charge from the opening hymn. In this case everyone involved—song leader, organist, pianist, ushers—will have planned the service with him and will look to him for their cues. They will be a bit edgy themselves, wondering if he will conduct the service in their accustomed format. Perhaps someone advises him in advance of "the way we usually do it," meaning, "We would like to continue this way, if you don't mind." If he is wise, he will thank them and follow their cues even while they are following his. If the only thing different is the face of the new leader, the congregation will more quickly feel at home with that new face. He may feel that many changes in format are needed, but not yet. The fewer the shocks and sharp turns in this first service, and indeed in many services to follow, the better.

I must reiterate that a common mistake of new pastors is to suppose that immediate and radical changes constitute the essence of taking charge. Somehow there is the feeling that if in any sense the format of the previous pastor is followed, the people will think the new man has no leadership style of his own. Perhaps they will think he is at sea. This is a mistaken perception. Taking charge doesn't require earthquakes and trumpets. The most skillful way to take charge is to slip into the driver's seat as quietly and unobtrusively as possible. People know he is there. They know he is the pastor. He does not have to advertise the fact. Sudden changes which may upset the music people and others and create a sense of confusion and uncertainty do not impress people favorably. Instead of imparting an impression of efficiency and competence, a windstorm of change suggests amateurishness. It is the nervous man, insecure and unsure, who feels that he must begin his leadership by flexing his muscles.

Study the church

This requires first of all becoming acquainted with the church as an organization—its officers, its finances, its methods, its strengths and weaknesses. A wise new pastor will take plenty of time to study the power structure—without anyone knowing what he is doing. Who dominates in the board meetings? Whose opinion carries the most weight? Not only in the church but in the community? What kind of people are they? What is the best way to work with them? Are they trustworthy?

But the pastor's knowledge should soon encompass everyone. He should early make a thorough study of the church roll. Who are these folk whose names have been removed? Where are they now? Why are they no longer in the church? (He may find some names of persons long since in heaven!) The Sunday school rolls also should be examined. The gap between last Sunday's attendance and the number of the roll—where are these people? Is any systematic contact being made?

A new pastor can do nothing smarter than to take his first month locating every family in his membership, and looking them in the eye in their homes if possible, or in some other setting if necessary. Learn their names, and as much personalia about them as possible. Without excessive or indiscreet prying he can gather information directly from them; they will be warmed and pleased by his interest. And certainly the names of children should roll easily off his tongue wherever he sees them. Just this much demonstration of human caring may tie a child to the church and save him for Jesus.

(Admittedly facility with names is very difficult for

some of us, almost at times our undoing. But we should
work at it. Young ministers, especially, should systematically cultivate a proficiency in this important link in
human relations.)

During this honeymoon stage—really, for at least a
year—the pastor should study the church in relation to
sociological types and classes. Schaller's books provide
much assistance in this.[2] While each church is unique,
each church can be categorized, at least tentatively. The
effort to study one's church in this way may enlarge one's
understanding so that the pastor will know where his
people are coming from and why they see things as they
do.

Above all, *Learn the facts.* The peril of sudden changes
is our ignorance of all the facts. We do not know the
background of some situations. If folk try to tell us, let
them. Be a good listener but then be mum. Don't walk
into a gossip trap. Some things a new pastor should
know; others he is just as well off not knowing. Great
wisdom is needed here and special discernment into the
hearts and minds of the people who are talking. Some
church members are so solid that full credence should be
given to what they say; they are imparting invaluable
insight. Others should be taken with a grain of salt—
indeed a whole salt shaker.

Unfortunately, some pastors, especially in the first
charge, tend to be naive in assessing character. As a
consequence they are easily taken in. Therefore, great
caution is in order. If a pastor can earn the confidence of
one or two established saints who clearly have both good
religion and good sense, it may be wise quietly and
noncommittally to draw them out. Learn their view of the
local situation and what they believe should be done.
Draw from them the perspective of experience. Gradually
the one or two can become several, until the pastor knows
he is surrounded by a team which he can trust and who

will work with him. One hopes these persons will be leaders already, board members or in other key positions. When after a year a new pastor knows he is flanked by a coterie of good and godly persons who will support him, he can begin to march more boldly. It is sad when he marches out too soon and looks around only to find himself alone.

Begin serving

Begin your ministry to people at once. And avoid posturing. Don't make grandiose predictions. Let the people rather see that serving is one's commitment. As soon as possible visit the sick and the aged. Become a familiar figure at the hospital. Bishop William A. Quayle's advice is still timely: "Get the impression prevalent in your congregation as speedily as may be after you become its pastor that you covet knowledge of all cases of sickness. Do not do this with a resigned air as of a martyr, but with an air as of a man who loves his people and whose privilege is in counseling them."[3]

One should be especially alert to the moves which might seem self-serving. If in the first few months a pastor shows more concern about a new parsonage and about salary than about people he is cutting his own throat. One man *within a month* after arrival persuaded the board to sell the very nice parsonage so that he could build his own house. Then he subcontracted the job himself at cut-rate costs by allowing merchants and suppliers to think that the church was building another parsonage. Naturally a few members got wind of his operation. As a consequence his ministry from then on was crippled by congregational restlessness and periodic blocs of negative votes which the poor man could never understand. But he had saddled himself from the beginning with a heavy load of quiet distrust. He made two mistakes: First, beginning with a major move in his own interests instead of demonstrating a spirit of service; and second, doing it in what appeared to sensitive laymen to be an underhanded manner.

Be affirming

The church may be torn by divisions, physically neglected and run-down, finances may be in the red and the people depressed and discouraged. But no matter how dark the situation, a new pastor can find something to praise and commend. The more lowering the clouds the more the pastor needs to find somewhere a silver lining and point to it, yet not in such a way as to call undue attention to their plight. Rather rebuild the people's hopes, their confidence, their self-respect. Commend, affirm, and then commend and affirm some more—their faithfulness, their giving, their singing, their very presence.

Easy does it

To bring this up again may seem unduly repetitious, but its importance justifies it. It is true that some of the problems may be—doubtless are—basically spiritual. Carnality may be deeply entrenched. Radical changes may be needed in key leadership positions. But for the present, ignore these facts as much as possible. Pray about them, quietly study them, and bide your time. God will bring about changes if the pastor prays enough and gives God room. Not every fence can be mended or old snag uprooted the first year. Nor can every change be made that cries out to be made. Some things require time and lots of it. In the meanwhile let us be patient with God, the people, and ourselves.

This does not mean turning our heads the other way. In extreme situations, such as moral messes, even a new pastor may have to wade in and take immediate action. But such demands are rare. What will irritate most will be the poor organist who thinks she owns the instrument, or a treasurer who thinks he owns the money, or Sunday school teachers who come late and unprepared—or maybe not at all. All of these obstacles to progress must in time be handled. But if a new pastor will wait until he has established his leadership, and has thoroughly melded himself into the affections of the people, and has come to a real grasp of the backgrounds and peripheral odds and ends of data not seen at first, he will then be able gradually and quietly to engineer changes and carry the church with him. And he can do it without getting the reputation of a manipulator. Patience is the name of the pastoral game.

Then he may be able to attend to special sore spots without alienating whole groups. Hardy C. Powers[4] once counseled me, "Remember that every person has his circle of friends and his sphere of influence. When you touch him [or her] you touch them. No matter how much of a headache some one person is, and how much some kind of action may be needed respecting him, you must keep in mind all those other people. Holding on to them may be important enough to justify putting up with the troublemaker. At least never discipline a person until you have weighed carefully the possible fallout."

Acquire pulpit respect

The pastor has come to be the preacher. He will lead, organize, plan, do many things; but unless he feeds the people they will not look up to him as they should and as they would like to. Folk will overlook many shortcomings and weaknesses if they learn that when Sunday morning and evening come they will not be wasting their time by going to church. If the new pastor tackles everything at once in the early months and in the process neglects his study and his books he will neutralize all his hustle and bustle.

Next to becoming known for godliness and integrity, establishing a reputation as a preacher the first year should be high on a pastor's agenda. People know this is the center of what he is there for, and if they find competence in the pulpit his influence will be strengthened in every other area. The beginner especially should capitalize on the very smallness of the church and the simplicity of the program to concentrate on learning to preach. I once heard Hugh Benner tell of his years in Santa Monica, California. The church was small enough for demands to be minimal. He devoted large amounts of time building sermons and learning to deliver them. A treasury was stored which became the foundation of his success in all subsequent assignments, culminating in the general superintendency of his church.

Hold steady when disillusioned

While the majority of churches are dominated by sincere Christians, many of them true saints, a church here and there will be a hotbed of carnal orneriness. An idealistic, enthusiastic, innocent young minister can walk into a hornet's nest of obstinacy, pettiness, quarrelsomeness, and just plain meanness. Just as men tend to idealize women and always suffer emotional trauma when they discover that women can be evil, so do budding theologues tend to idealize their first pastorate. Happy are they if they walk into the open arms of a loving, supportive church family. But if they find themselves being chewed alive by cats and tigers they may be so destroyed that with a crushed spirit they leave the ministry, never to return. Some form of preparation for the possible worst should be part of their mental and spiritual conditioning. A profound sense of call and a strong grip on God will be their only hope.

The famous Methodist evangelist John Church tells of his first pastorate. The bishop appointed him against the wishes of the church leaders, who determined to teach the bishop a lesson by starving the young couple out. No salary was paid and no food brought in. It was a critical moment. But John and his wife kept quiet, prayed (with more fasting than they preferred), held steady, called on the people and preached, until finally in some miraculous way the tide turned and in the end they were welcomed and loved. To have cut and run would have been costly for everyone.

A PASTOR'S PERCEPTION OF HIS ROLE

Let the pastor magnify shepherding. This is a matter of basic philosophy. Too many young pastors have been poisoned in their thinking before they even take their first charge. They dream of the megachurch, and do not want to settle into such a lowly role as shepherding a flock— that is mere "maintenance." They think only of leading a church that is exploding in size. How much this is promoted by a pure love of souls and how much of it by visions of grandeur only God knows. But if young pastors would stop drooling over the big churches, and stop reading everything they can get their hands on of spectacular success stories, and stop running to this and that seminar to find out how "it is done," and instead turn their undivided attention to the church they have, they might discover "acres of diamonds" in their own backyard.

These pastors or prospective pastors are getting the cart before the horse: They want to play Brahms before they have learned "Chopsticks." They want the large church before they have demonstrated their ability to handle the small church. Let them begin rather by paying attention to the people they have. Let them start loving *them*, with compassion and concern, and begin to ask God how they can better serve *them*, and it could be that by and by they will become the caliber of person God might trust with a megachurch, if such should be in God's blueprint.

Our perception of our role will affect, for good or ill, the way we take hold of a church. President J. Duane Beals of Western Evangelical Seminary adroitly summarizes the various models of the pastoral role which have been in vogue since World War II. First there was the fundamental shift from majoring on preaching to majoring on counseling. Unfortunately, this shift is still with us. Then there came the coach model of leadership, next the management-by-objectives model, next the servant-leader model. About this Beals comments, "Invariably the would-be servant-leader ends up as the slave to many masters." All of these models, he feels, are weighed in the balance and found wanting. He pleads for a return to the biblical model—that of shepherd. Shepherding includes managing and planning, but with the welfare of the sheep constantly in view. Shepherding is a kind of controlling which serves. Beyond business functions is a personal tie. The shepherd understands his sheep and loves them. He plans continually for a program which keeps them well fed, contented, and protected from enemies. The shepherd lives with his sheep, and he has no ambition to leave them for the palace on the hill.

Other things being equal, the man or woman who enters a new charge with this frame of mind is far more apt to be happy and to create a happy relationship with his or her people.

6

BREAKING THE BORDERLINE BARRIER

Pastors who honorably and faithfully stand by the stuff year after year in small pastorates demonstrate a commendable heroism and should not downgrade themselves. But in many cases, as they themselves would be the first to admit, their success is borderline. Their statistics swing narrowly between small minuses and small plusses. No dramatic turnarounds occur in their churches. Deep down they nurse the flicker of a feeling that they have potential for more extensive success—potential they have not learned how to tap.

How can a pastor who is borderline raise the level of his success? First, of course, there must be the humility of the learner. Second, he must have the intelligence to analyze weaknesses. Third, he must have the discipline required for change.

Generally borderline failure hinges not on goodness or badness, or sincerity or insincerity, or even native endowment. It hinges rather on an aggregation of *small faults which can be remedied if we determine to remedy them.* Surely any normally intelligent person, who applies himself diligently and with resolve, can learn to do the basic things which belong to his high calling, not just passably but well.

He or she can learn

—to speak properly and effectively;
—to look and act like a gentleman or lady (both in the pulpit and out);
—to be friendly and approachable;
—to master the functions of the ministry, such as weddings and funerals;
—to preside over public services and business meetings with poise and competence;
—to behave in homes so as to leave behind a holy fragrance;
—to manage finances so as to avoid reproach;
—to act like a Christian at home and toward the neighbors;
—to learn to work with people;
—to develop consistent, efficient and effective work habits.

Here are ten components of the pastorate. Serious flaws in any one of them can cast a shadow over all the others. One serious weakness may conceivably be so undermining as ultimately to bring down one's entire ministerial house upon one's head. Many pastors are needlessly faulty in several areas, apparently with no awareness of the offending flaws.

To be as helpful as possible, let us zero in on certain of the more crucial areas.

SHEDDING SUNDRY CRUDITIES

It is elementary that a pastor should know how to look and act like a gentleman or lady, whether in or out of the pulpit. Extreme faddishness but also dowdiness should be avoided. There should be neither teenage daring in dress nor hobo slovenliness. "Slovenliness," once said Oswald Chambers, "is an insult to the Holy

Ghost." No one needs to be sloppy, with uncombed hair or baggy clothes.

And it doesn't take a lot of effort to sit properly when in front of the people. When men slouch in their pulpit chairs, their legs wide apart (spread-eagle), or their legs crossed with a shoe resting on a knee, or wear drooping socks with the bare leg showing, they are advertising themselves as uninstructed, to say the least. If their people act the same, it probably matters little. But if people with some refinement and sense of propriety happen in they will mentally discredit the whole outfit. Professional persons who are with it are more respectful to the house of God, their congregation, and their calling.

This goes for street and town dress as well. One pastor would often amble to the post office of his small town with one suspender clinging precariously and the other dangling. His teenage daughter was embarrassed and the neighbors no doubt amused. And the image of the church was not enhanced.

All other offensive crudities should be weeded out. Not only do haircuts and ties need attention, but bad breath, stubbly face, unshined shoes, kiddish slang, illiterate speech ("Ya know," every ten words), and body odor. Such matters seem trifling perhaps, but they are often the very details which make the difference between the borderline man and the thriving pastor.

ACQUIRING A PLEASING PERSONALITY

Every pastor can learn to be friendly and approachable, whether in the restaurant or service station or store or at social events or in church. Persons who are overly reserved, dour, aloof, abrupt, and angular will have a hard time making friends and influencing people (especially if the previous pastor was laid-back, easy, and affable). Open, natural friendliness does not come easily with some pastors. They have to work at it. They do not need to become ebullient or garrulous, but they should learn to take the initiative, lay aside their natural shyness, put out their hand, and talk.

Even one's own people can unintentionally be held at bay by a detached manner of super busyness, rushing here and there, seemingly unmindful of them as persons. They get the feeling that he is too busy to talk to them. Let the pastor cultivate people awareness. Let him be everyone's friend and everyone's shepherd, not effusively or intrusively, but in such a way that people of any age or social status will feel free to approach him. One pastor I knew was so reserved and starchy that a lady member told my wife, "I could *never* go to him for counsel."

Yet preachers have at times tried too hard to be affable and have ended up being silly. This too can be one of the little flaws which lower a person's level of effectiveness. In one case the young pastor went so far in clowning at social events that he lost the respect of the men. The Christian men overlooked his kiddish antics because they loved him and believed in him, but several of the unsaved men stopped coming. A pastor should remember that his position is never less than pastor. His people expect him to be manly, discreet, and exemplary at all times—as well as affable. Even teenagers expect this down in their heart of hearts.

GOOD PEOPLE RELATIONS

Pastors will never get beyond borderline success and reach more fully their own potential unless they learn to get along with people. They must love them, understand them, feel for them. It isn't enough to work over people; we must work *with* them. Some pastors are wanting in tact. Their social radar is out of order, manners are missing. Incredible as it may seem, one pastor, when asked by his farm-wife parishioner if he could use a dozen eggs, snapped, "Pay your tithe, and I'll buy my own eggs." A misfit from day one, he didn't last long in the ministry.

A sensitivity to people can be cultivated. A pastor should be an assiduous student of human nature, not just in books but in his own people. He must learn to work with them as they are, not as he thinks they should be. Sister Jones is sensitive about her age. Brother Brown needs time to consider things; he doesn't handle surprises well. Brother Smith seems to need more pats on the back than others. He will do better if bolstered with generous amounts of affirmation and appreciation. Pastors who do not know how to make people feel good about themselves, but who are always rubbing the fur the wrong way and stepping on sensitive toes, will be finding themselves too close to that borderline for comfort.

IN THE HOMES OF PARISHIONERS

Surely a pastor can learn to behave in homes so as to leave behind a fragrance. We are talking now about conduct which contributes to the borderline situation. One pastor would breeze into a home and head straight for the refrigerator. "Got anything good to eat?" He thought that was the way to get next to the people. It wasn't. Another pastor sticks his shoes on the coffee table. Another picks up a magazine and thumbs through it while talking. Another prides himself on being casual in dress, and ends up being totally unprofessional, an embarrassment if the church member happens to have guests. Another pastor interrupts, argues, and is otherwise obnoxious. Another insists on hugging the little girls, not knowing that many little girls do not like to be hugged, not even by the pastor. Other pastors are indiscreet in timing their calls, in both senses: They come at the wrong time and/or stay too long. Still others are not sufficiently guarded against compromising situations. (Wise is the pastor who listens to his wife!) The consequence of all this is that no one takes these blunderbusses seriously.

A man or woman's appearance and deportment should at all times be such that if a neighbor should drop in the host or hostess can say with decent pride, "This is my pastor." The impression on children also should be constructive. To a great extent children form their perceptions of the ministry and develop their attachments (or aversions) during those special times when the pastor is in the home.

PULPIT GRACE

A pastor can learn to stand straight in the pulpit and speak with discipline and competence. He can study public speaking, voice control, mannerisms, and sufficiently improve in these matters that his people will not have reason to feel embarrassed. A pastor owes this much to his members. Proper pronunciation (which can be learned from a dictionary), clear enunciation, pleasant speed and volume, are all qualities which make the difference between a good and a poor speaker, which, in turn, will make the difference between a member's willingness to invite his neighbors and his reluctance to do so. In how many cases are such simple matters the culprits in the borderline situation?

When Gideon Williamson[1] was in his first pastorate, he had two annoying habits: one was sticking his hand in his coat pocket, the other was lifting his eyes above the people while preaching. When these habits were gently called to his attention by his wife, he was inclined to brush it off; surely he didn't do these things! But Mrs. Williamson cured the first habit by sewing up his pockets.

He soon learned not to reach for them. She cured the second by slipping up to the balcony a Sunday or two, and every time he looked up she waved at him. Breaking that habit didn't take long either. May we presume that Mrs. Williamson's alertness and resourcefulness, combined with his willingness to be corrected, might have had something to do with his future enlarged usefulness?

While the advice of Bishop Quayle was given to an earlier generation of preachers, it is perennially timely: "What attracts attention to a minister as being an uncouth demeanor is a misfortune, inasmuch as it distracts attention and brings thought to something other than the business of the hour, which is to worship the Living God." And he warns against "looking round on the congregation as if one were nervous lest the crowd would not be large." He must "be above the cheap feverishness of the size of a crowd."[2]

LEADERSHIP IN WORSHIP

Every pastor can learn to lead his people in public worship. This is more than proper posture and good speaking. It is spiritual leadership. This kind of leadership requires, first of all, good management of the service itself. If people are to worship, the service must be protected from haphazardness. An atmosphere of worship can be created when the service flows and each part is coherent with the whole. Angular, jerky distractions prevent worship. Other distractions include:

   a). Special singers clumping up from the back of the sanctuary to the mike.
   b). Loss of precious time manipulating the sound system.
   c). Excessive choreography and theatrics (we are here to worship, not watch).

d). Asking for ushers at the last moment; or, "Jim, where are the plates?"

e). Interjecting forgotten announcements (once heard between the "special" and the sermon: "Oh yes, I forgot to announce the basketball game Monday night").

f). Offertories that weaken the ceiling plaster (this goes for loud sound systems in general).

Many such forms of general disarray and noise "assault and battery" make it virtually impossible for the congregation to come into any real sense of the divine Presence. Let there be form without formality and reverence without starchiness. Warm amens and fervent testimonies do not hinder worship—they are elemental to it—but claptrap does. A plethora of novelties—sudden twists and turns, with surprise packages—will do the job very well of preventing worship. Of course if the purpose is entertainment and excitement, fine. Keep them guessing and watching.

Some pastors are overly afraid of ruts. A washboard road may prevent sleep, but after awhile it can become just as tiring as a rut. And if by "ruts" we mean a reasonably regular order of worship, the rut will not be the cause of deadness, only the accompaniment. And spiritual vitality is not recaptured by stunts and novelties.

This warning, however, should not be interpreted as meaning that no effort should be made to conduct a worship service in a lively and spirited manner. But the Spirit must be in it as well as spirit. "There is a difference," observed a wise old pastor, "between being spiritual and merely spirited." And awkward ineptness must be weeded out so that the Spirit will not be insulted or hindered.

Admittedly much of this depends partly on the other participants—the musicians, song leader, choir, special singers, ushers; but the pastor is in charge, and is in the long run responsible for achieving that degree of smoothness and finesse which makes worship at least possible.

Forms and approaches greatly vary. But some men are doing it these days with skill. Announcements are often given before the service proper begins. Music and prayer and offering and choir numbers are woven together into a beautiful tapestry. People find it easy to lift their hearts and minds in praise. They are carried along by a mood of receptivity and openness. They are ready for the preaching of the Word.

Required is careful training of all persons involved, meticulous planning for every detail of every service, and a harmonious spirit of teamwork between pastor and everyone who has any part at all in the hour.

But beyond organization and planning for worship lies a requisite so vital that without it the finesse will achieve little. *The pastor, himself, must worship,* both in front of his people and with them. This is difficult because of the burden of conducting the service. It becomes possible only (1) if the detail *has already been worked out* so that the service flows almost by itself; and (2) if the pastor is so prayed up that he is in a worshipful frame of mind. His own heart should be aglow with love for God. Otherwise his "worship" may be a charade.

I was once under the ministry of a young pastor who could take any limping service and make it leap with a sense of God's presence and power. No outlandish stunts or tricks. Few services he led failed to be experiences of renewal, with people going home feeling that they had touched God. But he was emotionally involved, not tackily but tastefully. He worshiped, often with tears on his cheeks. And he had a rare ability to sense just what a service needed at a particular moment. Need it be said that he came from the place of prayer?

The pastor who would conquer the borderline mal-
aise must learn the art of conducting meaningful public
worship services.

OTHER PUBLIC FUNCTIONS

Certain functions peculiar to the pastoral ministry
must be learned well. Primarily at this point I am thinking
of weddings and funerals. Details of form and procedure
can be studied in various manuals available. Since details
of funeral and burial practices vary in different parts of
the country, local customs can be learned from other
pastors, sometimes from morticians. If the pastor is not
sure, he should not hesitate to ask. A wise move would
be to attend a few funerals in the area to observe anything
unique about the procedure.

Weddings may require special study and practice.
Some pastors find weddings the scariest thing they do.
Other pastors glory in the wedding. Only the bride is
more regnant. If the scared and perhaps awkward and
unsure pastor will determine to master weddings and
funerals until he feels at home and can perform compe-
tently (though perhaps never without an occasional faux
pas), he will greatly bless his people and extend his reach
into the hearts and homes of the community.

MONEY MANAGEMENT (AGAIN!)

This is the second discussion of money in this book,
but the subject is so crucial that further attention is
justified. For failure here is a frequent contributor to the
borderline situation. A parsonage couple must learn to
manage their financial affairs. If they do not they will live
under the pressure and harassment of debt, fail to give
their best in service, and possibly bring reproach on both
themselves and the church.

If a couple just starting out in their first pastorate and

even before school bills are paid simply must have the best of everything—sterling silver, fine china, fancy car, etc.—they had either better pray for the demise of a rich uncle or start looking around for some other vocation. Spiritual depth will condition a couple to be willing gladly to live sacrificially in order to fulfill their calling.

It is not always the size of salary that makes the difference. Often it is management. Some couples make it fine (or at least "make it") on small salaries; others are perpetually in debt even on generous salaries. A couple should rigorously bring their spending urges to heel. They should fast and pray if need be until God helps them exercise discipline; and they should talk and talk until they can work out a viable management plan, then *together* work the plan. Let them not be ashamed to seek professional help in setting their financial house in order. It is absolutely imperative that they guard their credit and the good name of the church. A small used car is no disgrace. Unpaid bills are.

SOUND WORK HABITS

Most pastors feel worked to death. In actuality, they may not know the first ABC's of good work procedures. This too contributes to the borderline peril. These pastors accomplish little because they are not organized, not disciplined, and not knowledgeable in the management of time. They putter here and there, burn up a lot of gas, go through a lot of motions, but have little solid accomplishment to show for their busyness.

A president of a holiness college hired a middle-aged pastor as business manager. The pastor brought into his new position his customary casual off-and-on work habits. In contrast the president was at his desk every day from 8:00 to 12:00, and from 1:00 to 5:00. Everything else was as systematically under control as was his time. The disorganized pastor began to follow suit, though it was for him a new regimen. Gradually his productivity climbed. After some years he said to his boss, "I'm leaving. Now that I have learned to work, I want to take one more pastorate before retirement and see what I can do with my new 'know-how.'"

Admittedly there are demands in the pastorate that cannot always be compressed into a neat daily pattern. No one needs to be more flexible than the pastor. Yet most pastors could improve their productivity out of sight if they learned to work more efficiently. One successful pastor said, "I push my work; I don't let it push me."

Milo Arnold was sixty-four years of age when he was tapped by a new Bible College to be professor of pastoral theology. At that time he was pastor of a strong church. He had the verve, the commitment, the excitement, the enthusiasm of a man in his first pastorate. Since he had a daily devotional session on the local radio station he had nine talks and sermons per week to prepare. Yet he was faithful in calling, took part in the fun things, was attentive to his wife, enjoyed life, and in addition wrote books! But he took six 4 x 6 cards each Sunday afternoon and mapped out his hourly tasks: the calls that should be made, errands to be run, meetings, study sessions, for each day of the week. On Monday morning he took Monday's card and started out. Simple. Of course he had interruptions. But he would get right back on the track, and had the time of his life doing it.

Sound work habits include wise priorities as well as a disciplined schedule. An elder recently confided to me that his last pastorate of ten years was so wobbly, in spite of hard work, that he stepped aside to secular employment, but began attending a church where powerful preaching and strong teaching are building a strong congregation. Quietly he said, "I see now that I did not really feed my people. My priorities were not in order."

Gordon Wetmore,[3] when a Kansas City pastor, explained his priorities to a young seminarian. He said, "They are Prayer, Preparation, and People." Even people must not be allowed to infringe on prayer and preparation. For if prayer and preparation are neglected, the people themselves will be deprived.

These are some cliff-hangers in the pastoral ministry. Some pastors are not producing as they know they should and could because they have not given sufficient attention to these crucial areas. If they will resolutely study themselves and their weaknesses, map out a plan for improvement, and persistently follow through with their plan, they will discover that they have turned a corner and entered a new and exciting ministerial world. Bon voyage!

7

THE MINISTRY WITH STAYING POWER

The staying power needed is twofold: the ability to remain in the ministry for life and the ability to succeed in one place over a number of years. The ministerial turnover in today's church world prevents maximum depth in pastoral relations and maximum impact on church communities. When pastors dedicate and marry one generation and start on the next, the affectional and emotional bonds cemented constitute a potent influence in molding and nurturing the families in his care, including children, youth, parents and grandparents. Such a pastor is a cohesive force in the social fabric of the church and its entire constituency.

SEEING IT THROUGH

Longer, not shorter

Perhaps it is time to learn to think in terms of extended ministries. James D. Glasse suggests that when a pastor is tempted to say to himself, "I have been a pastor of this church for five years; perhaps it is time for me to move on," he should imagine these words in the mouth of the local lawyer, teacher, or physician, then ask

himself if such a soliloquy for *them* would make sense.[1]
Perhaps it does not for him either.

Lyle Pointer urges that longer pastorates be treated as
a "criterion of success." He reports that a personal study
of the 1,300 churches in his denomination that do not
report any new members by profession of faith revealed
that sixty percent of them were barren because of pastoral
turnover. He says, "The strongest variable in people
joining the church is the stability and care of a pastor."[2]

Upward, not downward

Getting off to a good start makes lasting success
easier and more likely. However, some men seem peculiarly gifted in making good starts, but have a strange
habit of blowing it down the line. A ministry in a
particular place should be stronger at the end than in the
beginning. When it is really time for a pastor to leave, he
should leave in a blaze of glory not in a fizzle or a
whimper. The ascending line of rapport and productivity
need not be absolutely free from dips, but it should
become steadier and firmer with time. The pastor and his
people should increasingly blend into one spiritual force
for the advancement of Christ's kingdom.

Unfortunately, in some cases the "oneness" is the
inertia of a stalemate. Former tensions are gone only to be
replaced by ennui. The fire has burned out. The anticipa-
tion and excitement of a church going places for God and
holiness are dissolved into the languid acceptance of a
dead-end status quo. Both sides of the equation are
marking time: the pastor for a miracle, a call elsewhere, or
retirement; the church for the same—but with less faith
for a miracle.

How can a man continue to be a growing, enthusiastic, and effective producer five, ten, fifteen, even twenty
years in one place? It surely does not need to be said that

he must keep growing as a person and as a leader. By toil and discipline he must acquire real intellectual and spiritual depth. Furthermore, he must come to know his people so well that he knows what will work and what will not; where they will follow and where they will not. And his love for them and theirs for him must be a growing thing. His walk among them must remain untarnished by trickiness or manipulation or moral shadow. Their faith in his personal holiness of character should be more sure after ten years than it was after one. As their shepherd, his care for them in times of grief and trouble will have been repeatedly confirmed at countless bedsides and in hurting homes.

Such a progressive fruitfulness will require not only personal holiness but a flexibility and openness to new ideas. The pastor must be able to adjust methods and concepts to changing times and changing needs. He can do this without wavering in his basic commitments and without compromising denominational integrity.

A character flaw?

If a man begins his ministry still beset by the character weakness of copping out, he had better take his character in hand and get rid of that weakness. Only disciplined men will make it.

A case history may underscore the point. A minister of my acquaintance has a long history of numerous jobs and sudden changes. His trait has been to take a job with great gusto and produce glowing results the first year. Then his enthusiasm wanes and paranoia takes over. This is followed before long by an impulsive, untimely resignation. He seems to have to be carried along by the tide of the dramatic and buoyed by the excitement of newness. His penchant for the dramatic has its last fling in the impetuous way he resigns and gets out. It seems that nothing can be done normally, quietly, deliberately, but always with some sort of fanfare and melodrama.

What are the character weaknesses we see working here? For one thing, he lacks the disciplined commitment which holds him to the task when the drive of initial enthusiasm is used up. The excitement of a new job has great propulsive power, but such power is soon exhausted. In this case, the capacity for sustained labor, which must take over when the initial thrust has spent itself, is lacking. He is unable to apply himself, day after day, to the humdrum. This is a serious character flaw.

This good man exemplifies a second character defect. This is the failure to master the know-how of one's job below the level of personality flair. Underneath the crest of riding high are undertows which must be managed. Beneath the hood of a powerful car are nuts and bolts that a driver must understand if he would succeed in the grueling long-distance test run. The pastoral ministry is a complex affair that some men seem never to master beyond the horns and bunting.

But the most revealing character weakness, seen too often unfortunately, is a fundamental self-centeredness. This is hidden from its possessor; in fact in most cases the accusation would be met by shocked and outraged denial. But the self-centeredness is demonstrated by the ease with which some men can leave a hurt and puzzled flock. There is little unselfish love which thinks first of all of the welfare of the sheep. There is little sign of the shepherd's heart. A profound sense of responsibility to *this* place, to *these* people is lacking. Instead of seeking to lead them into greener pastures, the pastor seeks greener pastures for himself.

When one young pastor fresh out of college met his church board for the first time, one of his men said to him, "What do they teach you fellows at college, anyway? To use these little churches as a stepping-stone to

something better? To get in and out as fast as you can?"
Then with great intensity he challenged, "Are you going
to stay?" The church was in a poor building, in the wrong
part of an inner city, with a few discouraged members,
and with a record of about a dozen pastors in eighteen
years. The young man knew how unpromising and
almost hopeless the situation was. But he said, "I'll stay."
And he did. It took a long while to make even a dent, and
another substantial time frame to turn the church around,
but when he moved nine years later he left behind one of
the strongest churches on the district. He is now into his
twelfth year of his second pastorate.

THE DEADLY PERIL OF PRESSURE

If we are to develop a ministry with staying power,
we must learn to live with pressure. A pithy truism is
"There is no success without stress." This is true because
if one is to succeed he must put his whole weight against
obstacles to success. A more familiar form of expression is
the saying that one must put his shoulder to the wheel.
But sometimes the boulders blocking the wheel are
people. At other times financial pressures seem like
insurmountable blockades. To make progress the pastor
must continually be leaning against the enterprise. In the
process of putting pressure on others, they put pressure
on him. Tension results. Ideally the pastor should be able
to apply reasonable pressure without tension building up
in his own psyche. But for most of us that is expecting
what is difficult if not impossible. How are we going to
handle this inward tension? How can we avoid the
inevitable stress from destroying us, and perhaps even
tearing down what we are so earnestly trying to build up?
Before attempting an answer to this question, perhaps we should seek to identify the various sources of
pressure. At this point we will mention two (others later).

Denominational pressures

These are from the top down, from church leaders, departments, executives, and superintendents. These pressures are enormous. The pastor feels that his statistics are being minutely scrutinized, and that they determine almost totally the denomination's evaluation of him. This evaluation, he believes, will control his future opportunities. Therefore he feels driven, almost to the point of desperation, either to adopt a cynical, no-care attitude and start vegetating, or to find some way, whatever it may be, to achieve at least a show of success. A gradual increase in hype and decrease in depth may result.

That the pastor's apprehension has some basis in fact must be admitted. But what is more crucial is that his perception of the structure and its dynamics is both exaggerated and askew. His uptightness is more self-generated than denomination-generated. His concern for growth should be his own, not impressed upon him by others. In fact his own internal pressure for souls should exceed anything imposed on him from above. If it is, he will be more apt to see the schemes and plans generated elsewhere as welcome aids, not as cruel whips.

Furthermore, the pastor should understand the real motivation of his leaders. Leaders of holiness denominations do not really want statistical growth at any cost. Certainly not at the cost of personal integrity or church doctrines. But leaders know that most people do their best work under pressure, and without pressure some will do virtually nothing at all. They desire by various means to provide incentives, and, if necessary, goads to elicit from a man his best.

Because of the open nature of the ministry, and because with most of us as our paunchiness grows our pace slows, we tend to lose the fervor of our youthful enthusiasm and drift toward dead center. Here we may rock along in less-than-our-best doldrums for years. When we are young, scared, and hungry, we are driven to pray mightily and work hard. But in middle life, when we "have it made" in a nice parsonage and comfortable salary, when we no longer dream of being a district superintendent, and when we know that any vote of our name for general office would be a case of mistaken identity, we tend to settle on our lees. One district superintendent asked me, "How can I get these comfortable middle-aged men to do anything? How can I spark new fire and vision?" Yet generally in preacher get-togethers these are the ones who will bewail the emphasis on numbers. And these are the ones for whom some degree of pressure from above is a human-nature kind of necessity.

Parish pressures

These are the strains and demands which are inherent in any local church, by its very nature. Endless decisions press in on a pastor's day. The constant jangling of the phone, the almost daily complaint of some offended soul, the ups and downs of attendance, the irregularity and undependability of teachers and other workers, the burden of making ends meet, the difficulty of finding uninterrupted time for study, the many meetings almost weekly, the delinquent budgets, the looming annual conference or assembly, and dozens of such ubiquitous concerns wear a man down and in the process of wearing him down key him up.

Only a pastor can understand the pressure inherent in the inescapable regularity of three services each week. One week is no more than ended when the next three public obligations begin bearing down on him. He cannot postpone them, evade them, or run and hide. As children call out, "Here I come, ready or not," these relentless demands compel his time, energies, and attention, and then force him to perform when many times he feels totally unprepared and incapable—all this plus the myriads of activities in between. Other strains are added by family problems, money needs, perhaps limited health.

It is no wonder that pastors and their wives tend to break down in the early years of their ministry. If they can weather this rough-water period and learn to manage their pressures, they will in the end prove good insurance risks. In fact, they will probably live a long time.

But the parsonage couple must learn to handle stress before too much damage is done. It is in the nature of stress to be cumulative. It is self-magnifying. It is also in the nature of stress to seek ventilation. This is why safety valves are put on steam engines. The peril is in allowing our stress to be ventilated on our families or show in our sermons or in official meetings. We do not intend to do this, it is just that these entities happen to be handy and convenient when we let off a little steam.

Tension fouls up our view of things. Our feelings are unreliable and our judgment becomes distorted. Our tension begins to show in the edginess of our sermons. We start blaming, pushing, shoving. The greater becomes our tension the more rigid and angular our methods become. Since things don't seem to be working, we are determined to make them work, and in the process unwittingly begin tearing things apart. In the end we find ourselves burning down the forest in order to get at the underbrush.

LEARNING TO LIVE WITH PRESSURE

How can pastors learn to self-perceive this state of mind? And how can they learn to relax and bring everything back into perspective before the damage is done? How can they release their tensions in a renewing and constructive way instead of in a destructive manner?

Guard the vision

How vivid and bright it was when we first started! We were electrified by the sweep of the noblest calling on earth. We saw ourselves winning lost men and women to Christ, nurturing them in the faith, guiding and counseling them, steadying them on their way to heaven. But somewhere along the line we found ourselves trying to put out petty fires and the smoke began to obscure the far horizon. We became preoccupied with the nitty-gritty. Life seemed to be an endless series of mundane duties which bore no discernible relation to the noble accomplishments we had envisioned for the ministry. The nuts and bolts of running a church gradually but insidiously robbed us of our enthusiasm.

As an artist frequently backs off from his easel in order to keep before him the whole picture, so must we continually refocus our vision. If even a cup of cold water has its reward (Matt. 10:42), then we may be sure that nothing we do in the pastorate, no matter how humdrum or menial, no matter how routine, whether contracting a church plumbing job or mowing the church lawn, is lost motion, if done in love and in the spirit of Jesus. Every action has a flow of unseen influence which the Holy Spirit draws into the heart of things. The so-called "nuts and bolts" become pieces of mosaic which God works into His authentic pattern of ministry.

Accept the challenge

When problems are seen as challenges there is a certain thrill and excitement about tackling them. Even the ringing of the phone can come through as an exciting bit of the day, each ring carrying its own mystery, its own potential for service, even adventure. Implicit in it is a golden opportunity for being wise—right now—in response; of being a loving shepherd with genuine interest and concern. The call may prompt a hospital trip, a home visit, or reveal some other crisis. But always the challenge is there, which a competent pastor faces with a certain joy and exhilaration.

Be mature

Much internal pressure builds up from our immature reactions. We as ministers can be as petty as our people in our magnification of the trivial. Can we sort out life intelligently? Do we keep small things small or allow them to assume mountainous proportions, until they threaten to crush us?

The surest evidence of maturity is our ability to laugh. Pastors without a sense of humor will bury themselves in the grave of their own grimness. The parsonage should be a jolly place. At times, so should vestries where business meetings are conducted. Pastors who can laugh at themselves and with others, who can see the amusing side of the human scene, will shed their tensions as they go along. The laughing man is not normally the uptight man. Neil Wiseman reports that one retired pastor said, "If I had my ministry to do over, I would enjoy it more."

Be realistic

Every pastor must sooner or later come to terms with the realities of human limitation. No man worth his salt will ever lie down at night completely satisfied with what he has been able to get done that day. Unmade pastoral calls, unanswered correspondence, and unsolved problems will haunt him. It is proper for him to be forever on the prowl for improved methods whereby the quantity of work can be increased. But no matter how much he improves there will always be the day's leftovers. This will drive him either out of the ministry or to an early grave, if he cannot learn to live with this fact of life with inner peace of mind and without guilt-lashings.

James D. Glasse speaks of pastors' attempts to play God by supposing that if they just work hard enough they can do everything for everybody. But this is unrealistic. "It should be enough," observes Glasse, "to point out that God himself . . . created the heavens and the earth in six days—and took a day off. Some pastors act as if they feared the creation would come to a halt if they took a day off."[3]

Avoid excessive fatigue

The important word here is "excessive." Some degree of fatigue will be a frequent experience if we are on the job. As Don Wellman has wisely observed, "We are going to get tired anyway, so we may as well get tired in the Lord's work." If therefore our weariness is healthy at the end of the day, we will feel good about ourselves and sleep well. But excessive weariness cripples us, for no one can think straight or perform up to par when exhausted. Some persons *seem* to be able to, but only for a short time; then efficiency plummets. Being a workaholic is great, up to the point of one's physical resources. But the man who habitually borrows energy from tomorrow will ultimately have to repay with high interest. Therefore every pastor must find his own way to achieve physical, nervous, and emotional renewal. He must learn how to unwind, to really rest, and for the moment at least get out from under the load. This may involve leaving town, going to bed for a day, golfing, playing games, going fishing, taking his wife out for a nice meal and spending the evening just visiting *with each other*. (Most wives would vote for this!)

Go to prayer

While all of these ways of handling stress are valid, in the end the problem can best be solved on our knees. Therefore, the best way to handle the stresses of the ministry and to avoid spilling them all over the place, is deliberately to *empty them in the prayer closet.* This is where they should all be brought. If we first take them out on God, we will be less apt to take them out on people. Let all our pent-up anxieties and disappointments be vented on our knees. But we must stay there until the catharsis has done its work. We must touch God to such a degree that we actually do cast our burden on the Lord, and can literally emerge *without it.* Then we can go back to the pressures themselves with poise and joy. The stresses have lost their sting. They no longer can be used by the devil as a cat-o'-nine-tails. And we can move quietly and calmly through our work knowing that a Higher Power has taken over. The power of the Spirit in us has been renewed.

8

THE REAL BURNOUT CULPRITS?

The problem of stress with its frequent consequence, burnout, is so acute that we cannot yet drop it for other matters. In the previous chapter we identified two major sources of stress: denominational and parish pressures. These are inherent in the nature of the job and are inescapable. Perhaps they might be called occupational hazards. But in this chapter we wish to identify other causes of stress which are not occupational hazards but personal distortions.

SELF-GENERATED CAUSES

Wise is the pastor who sees that the most deadly forms of stress are those which are self-generated. Hard work, responsibility, and problems, in and of themselves, do not usually bring breakdown. Pastors and their wives are destroyed when the work and problems are mixed with three other elements which together create a poison-ous brew. The first is cognitive—wrong beliefs—and may be innocent, but still devastating. The second is simply a matter of bad managerial judgment: unrealistic goals. The third element is not innocent but carnal. It is contaminat-ed ambition. When the denominational pressures and built-in pressures of a local church are combined with wrong beliefs, misguided goals, and self-centered motives the result is (to change the figure) a boiling cauldron. However, it is not necessary for all three to be present for the damage to be done. Any one of the three can destroy a pastor.

Also, it should be conceded that insecurity, with its defensiveness and uptightness, may and often does arise solely out of inexperience. The preacher is scared and unsure of himself. Time will remedy this. As his know-how improves and his understanding matures, his self-confidence will grow, and he will be able to operate in a relaxed mode—for which everyone will be thankful. But let us get back on track.

Wrong beliefs

The *wrong beliefs* are never articulated, i.e., they are not held consciously and verbally. They are lurking assumptions at the subliminal level. They are misconceptions concerning the real nature of the pastor's relationship with his people and his job. These pastors are infected with the notion, for one thing, that they are supposed to be infallible and that their people expect them to be infallible. Furthermore, they fear that any demonstration of their fallibility will result in the loss of their ability to lead and loss of respect. They think that opposition always implies a dislike of them personally and a rejection of their leadership; that negative votes mean the end of the road. Many concurrent false suppositions could be mentioned, but these will suffice to give the picture. These are wrong beliefs, every one.

Pastors never declare, "I am infallible." They only assume the fact. This assumption is demonstrated by the spontaneous shock and irritation they feel when their judgments are challenged. Professional maturity will minimize if not totally eliminate such feelings.

Pastors should consider the medical doctor. They make mistakes (even fatal ones) but do not lose faith in themselves as good doctors. Doctors lose patients to other doctors, but they go right on practicing. Most of them manage these embarrassments with reasonable equanimity and good sense. They understand that it is all part of the dynamics of the human situation. Pastors also must learn to roll with the punches and realize that God's work is held together by God himself. The pastor who can accept his mistakes and admit them, who can acknowledge and live with his limitations, and look to the God whom he is serving, and remember that "except the Lord build the house, they labor in vain that build it" (Ps. 127:1, KJV) can learn to sleep in peace at night. Some things must be committed to God and to time.

It will bear repeating that nowhere is a zestful sense of humor, including the ability to laugh at one's self, more essential than in the ministry. Some pastors take themselves too seriously. It is good to take their work seriously, but not themselves. Many times will come when a pastor feels let down, chagrined, embarrassed, maybe set back on his heels—but he should view these experiences as simply par for the course. His personal sense of worth and security must be sufficiently well grounded and sturdy to weather all such. And let him remember the advice of Helmut Gollwitzer: "No man can learn from experience who does not allow it to humble him."[1] It may humiliate him without humbling him. The person who is merely humiliated is still looking for an out. He is still resorting to rationalizations. When he is humbled he faces squarely his own responsibility, and as a consequence, can turn the unpleasant experience into a learning experience.

Some pastors never really learn. One man served

four different churches and claimed twenty years' experience. His friends commented that he really didn't have twenty years' experience, only five years' experience repeated four times.

Unrealistic goals

"Unrealistic goals is another contributor to burnout," writes one district superintendent. Pastors fail "to set specific perimeters of ministry area and endeavor." They try to accomplish too many things in too short a time. Or they commit themselves publicly to statistical goals which sensible analysis would label as foolhardy. Every time a pastor announces specific numerical goals he puts his credibility on the line. They should be well within the range not just of possibility but probability so that in the mind of everyone success in reaching them can be a reasonable expectation. Every such success is an exciting morale booster, whereas every failed goal sends morale plummeting into the cellar. Too many such failures brands a pastor as an impractical dreamer and ineffective leader.

Publicly ballyhooed goals tend to paint a man into a corner. As the year races toward district assembly or conference and the goals are not being met, the pastor begins to panic. He looks for a way out of his trap. Nothing feeds internal pressure more than feeling driven by goals which are becoming more and more elusive. The poor pastor struggles harder, which only tightens his solar plexus and encourages the undertaker. Meanwhile, the people become more goal-resistant. They no longer respond to his announcements with enthusiasm, and increasingly view him as a sweet, well-meaning bungler.

CONTAMINATED AMBITION

What about *contaminated ambition*? Healthy ambition is a drive to accomplish something worthwhile. Holy ambition is the drive to accomplish this something for God. But the ambition becomes contaminated and compromised when self begins to reign. These preachers, much more profoundly than they are willing to see, are too much enamored with position, prestige, and power. This leads to, and generally includes, some degree of sniveling, shriveling envy. Then soreness over so-called dirty deals or missed promotions begins to blister the soul.

These pastors accuse their denomination of being numbers conscious, but they fall into that trap themselves, and dig a hole deeper than anyone's. They think in terms of size—salary, membership, attendance; and habitually filter surrounding churches through these criteria. Let them not cast the first stone!

Several signs suggest that in some cases the real problem may be an unsanctified ego.

a. *The pastor's fervor has become fever*. He is chronically uptight. He tries too hard.
b. *He plays the angles*. He worms his way into the right circles and manages to get on the right side of the right people.
c. *He resorts more and more* to Madison Avenue methods and less and less to the prayer closet.
d. *He is overly conscious of his competition*. I watched one pastor of a city church as he fidgeted around his office during the Sunday school hour. He was in fierce rivalry with the pastor downtown, and was like a cat on a hot tin roof over the attendance statistics that day. He kept opening the door a crack to see what the crowd looked like. This kind of "drive" is fleshly and small-minded. And

horribly enslaving. In addition it is a travesty on
the ministry.

e. *Paranoia sets in.* These insecure, self-centered,
fearful pastors, full of rivalry and anxiety, too
conscious of their pecking order or spot on the
totem pole, begin to smell a rat when there is
none. They imagine opposition that does not exist.
They misinterpret every little circle of talking
friends. If a board member raises a question, the
pastor suspiciously demands, "Why did you ask
that?" They plant spies in the church family to
report what is going on. If there are "no" votes an
apparatus is stealthily set in place with a few "in
folk" to find out the culprits.

Planting spies and otherwise putting one clique
against another is a scenario for disaster. Only
pathetic insecurity coupled with cynical distrust
will operate on this low level. If there are sparks of
unrest such paranoiac behavior will create a roar-
ing conflagration which will seriously damage if
not completely destroy the church.

f. *Driving imperialism* is very apt to characterize these
pastors. Admittedly this may be immaturity or
temperament, not necessarily carnality. But in any
case these persons are overly autocratic in the way
they try to ramrod their plans through. One pastor
of a mid-size church, old and somewhat set in its
ways, attended a Jack Hyles bus ministry seminar.
Sunday morning back in his home church he
preached a bellowing and bellicose sermon on the
bus ministry, declaring, as he left the pulpit and
walked the aisles, "We are going to have a bus
ministry whether you people like it or not." Well,
some laymen love a good fight. Within three
months he was out.[2]

Therefore, while at times the primary culprit in burnout is a flock of misconceptions in one's basic philosophy, or some self-trapping snares in method, at other times (we fear) there is an unsanctified ego in the way. These men need to take their own sermonic medicine. They preach dying out to their self-seeking laymen; now let them die out themselves. No pastor past the enthusiasms of the early years can remain happy in the ministry unless he has been delivered totally from carnal ambition—and its contrail, bitterness.

Being "dead" does not mean one no longer prefers praise to blame, or that blame will no longer sting. Nor does it mean that we are never tempted to wish for larger opportunities. But it means that we do not live for praise; and it means that we are not immobilized by the smallness of our church. Our sense of self-worth has a higher source. Our vision is of God and holy things, and we are excited about the privilege of being where we are, loving *these* people, helping *them,* and preaching in *this place* the gospel of the living Christ. In thus rejoicing in our present ministry we magnify our calling.

Surely our love for God and our dedication to our task should match that of the famed pianist Arthur Rubenstein. His son said that when giving himself to his music his absorption "was pure—devoid of self." There are human, secondary motivations in the pastorate, to be sure. But is there not also a level of pure joy and devotion and love which is "devoid of self"?

LOVE, THE ANTIDOTE TO STRESS

We have already spoken of prayer as the way par excellence to defuse the stresses and tensions of the ministry. An even deeper, more basic effect of prayer is a fresh baptism of love for our people. The truth of the matter is many pastors love success but they do not love people. Not really. They think they love people but it is in the abstract. They feel no deep, warm, vibrating, tender, jovial, sympathetic love for *these* people. This is why they are so easily upset by them. Thin love fosters thin nerves.

Some pastors are like the bachelor professor who was always lecturing the neighborhood mothers, "Don't spank! Just love the child!" One evening he caught one of the neighborhood tykes stepping in the newly laid cement of his backyard walk. Rushing out he snatched the child up and was about to lay a heavy hand on its bottom when the lady next door called out, "Oh, Professor, don't spank, just love the child!" His retort was, "I do love the child in the abstract but not in the concrete." Some preachers love humanity in the abstract but not in the concrete situation near at hand. Their sentimental eloquence is about the poor, but they do nothing for the poor family on the corner. They are burdened, in the abstract, for lost souls, but do not win their neighbor.

There is nothing like a deep prayer life for the correction of this superficiality and professionalism; and in the process, prayer becomes the answer to the problem of stress. God can enable the pastor to say with Paul, "For Christ's love compels us" (2 Cor. 5:14). When Christ's love compels, His grace enables. "I can do everything through him who gives me strength" (Phil. 4:13).

9

DOING GOD'S WORK GOD'S WAY

Every pastor must decide early in his ministry whether he will operate "in the flesh" or "in the Spirit." One young pastor returned from a seminar put on by big business teaching the secrets of management for growth. He boasted to his friends, "I have learned how to develop a superchurch." He began to operate on this level, enlisting prestigious names, setting up vanity banquets, stroking egos. But after a year the enterprise fell apart, and someone else had to pick up the pieces.

Another pastor knew the lines of Spirit-power and guidance. On Sunday morning he had the congregation kneel for prayer. After he had prayed he said, "Let us remain in prayer. I feel God is speaking to someone today." He didn't know that at that moment a young man, a high school senior in the back row of the choir was in the throes of a struggle, sensing that God was calling him to preach. In the time given by the pastor, he said yes to God. When they arose the pastor said, "I feel the Holy Spirit wants someone to speak." The young man stood and confessed to his call. In the congregation were several high school buddies who had attended at the young man's invitation. At the close of the sermon every one of them sought God at the altar. It was the beginning of a life of rare usefulness, including high office in his denomination—because there was a pastor who knew how to operate in the Spirit.

A truly Spirit-filled pastor desires to please God in his methods and do God's work in God's way. He will therefore not depend on the promotional schemes of the world, for he is aware that the "weapons we fight with are not the weapons of the world. On the contrary, they have divine power to demolish strongholds" (2 Cor. 10:4). While there are continuities with the secular world in organizational and administrative functions, the discontinuities are more profound. The pastor operates in a different order of reality from that of the world.

Pastoral work is multifaceted, involving administration, counseling, and public ministrations. But in the hustle and bustle of the modern parish the three functions most commonly neglected are in fact the most fundamental to lasting success. They are prayer, preaching/teaching, and pastoral calling (see chapter 10). These are not the easiest activities of the ministry; rather they are the most difficult. Giving the attention to prayer, preaching, and calling which the work demands requires enormous stocks of discipline and great reservoirs of patience. It requires a depth of commitment not always possessed. It requires sound theological underpinnings. There must be no mental fog concerning the nature of the ministry and the spiritual dynamics which belong to it. The pastor must be a *believer* in every atom of his being. Erwin W. Lutzer is right:

> Results in themselves are not a proof that God is pleased. It is possible to win attendance contests and disseminate the Gospel and see results; all these activities can be done without pleasing God! Such results can be achieved by deceptive gimmicks or for purely personal satisfaction. It is not enough to do God's work; it must be done in His way and for His credit.[1]

The pastor who would do God's work God's way must see that the ministry without the supernatural dimension—without the immediate and pervasive power of God—is but a juggler's performance. He must have no haziness about the primacy of the sin problem (it is not mental illness); the power of the Holy Spirit to awaken, regenerate, and sanctify; the power of the preached Word as the Spirit's catalyst in all of this. He must be willing to labor on his knees, at his desk, and in shoe leather. And he must be willing for the cutting edge of his labors to be more invisible than visible for disconcerting blocks of time; yet steadfastly to believe that God is making his ministry quietly effective on the spiritual level of life, the level without fanfare, where glorious discoveries of life-changing fruit are often sparsely spaced between barren stretches when it seems nothing is going on.

This kind of applied pastoral theology will occasionally be honored by the Spirit in outbreaks of real revival. Such revival will not depend on banquets, guest artists, singing and jigging groups, or other sundry religious entertainers. It will be a moral awakening. People will discover that their big problem is not jobs or self-esteem or acceptance in a "caring" church, but sin. The Holy Spirit will prompt repentance, confession, restitution, radical newness of lifestyle. Families will be reunited. Alcoholics and other addicts will be delivered. There will be profound upheaval, the reconstructive kind, in both church and community. Then for a time rapid growth will occur, but this will be of God rather than of the flesh.

If such a revival can be harnessed by wise leadership to new directions in total church life, with less emphasis on fun and games and a greater participation in prayer meetings and a clearer vision of a truly spiritual program, the result will be not only permanently stronger Christians but an atmosphere of continuous revival. This is the healthy state, and should be the aim and goal of every pastor. But these mountain peaks of blessing and the higher elevations which follow will be God's answer to the months and years of steady plodding in prayer, calling, and preaching.

THE PLACE OF PRAYER

In the previous chapter we saw prayer as the best antidote to stress. But it is much more than a safety valve or a means of personal renewal. It is also our arsenal for attack. It is the most effective mode of wresting souls from the enemy and winning victories for the kingdom.

In Luke 5:16 we read that Jesus "often withdrew to lonely places and prayed." In the next verse we are told that "the power of the Lord was present for him to heal the sick." Private prayer, public power—this is the divine order. If it was for Jesus, how much more will this be the order for us. To pray well is to work well.

But the praying that will make the difference is more than sleepily hanging our head over a wishing well. It is the kind of praying which Satan will marshall all hell to stop. It takes time, energy, determination, and discipline. It is praying in the Spirit, which is prayer in harmony with the Spirit and enabled by the Spirit. It becomes a vehicle for the torrential intercessions of the Spirit. But when pastors pray like that wonderful things happen.

One pastor of my acquaintance spent two hours every morning before breakfast in prayer. Not by fits and starts, but as a life pattern. He was not bursting with personal charisma. There was no flashy brilliance. He was an ordinary sort. But God helped him build a strong church which is today one of the sturdiest in the Midwest. Admittedly not everyone is capable of such a rugged prayer regimen. But even an hour would make a telling difference.

Subjective effects

Prayer will make the difference between church work carried out in the energy of the flesh and church work done in the power of the Spirit. The daily routine will have the touch of fire upon it. A word of wisdom here, a special guidance there, will mark a man's ministry with a heavenly aura. If he ever experiences burnout, it will be purely physical; it will not be because the romance of the ministry has been lost. Prayer is the panoply against dry rot (and other kinds of rot, too!). It keeps the pastor going with holy radiance. He is a marked man— marked by faith, joy, and optimism in spite of droughts and setbacks.

In prayer the pastor will be given courage to be faithful and to deliver the difficult sermon and face the painful confrontation. In prayer he will be given ideas and concerns for preaching, not as an exemption from arduous toil but as a sense of direction. And prayer will assure the pastor of anointing when he stands up to deliver the message God has given him.

In prayer the pastor will be given wisdom for the seemingly impossible situation. He will learn how to wait, perhaps be silent. He will come to understand his own faults and weaknesses and be given grace to overcome them. He will receive ideas, insights, solutions, plans, methods—far more workable, for him, than those acquired at seminars.[2] For these plans will be custom-designed for him and his church.

Objective effects

The power of prayer does not end with the pray-er, but extends through the direct action of the Holy Spirit to people and situations which need changing. Why God does some things in answer to prayer that He does not do without prayer is a fact in the divine economy which we do not altogether understand. John Wesley reasons this way: "If you (because you have a regard for me) would do more for a third person at my request than otherwise you would have done, how much more will God, at the request of his beloved children, give blessings to those they pray for, which otherwise he would not have given!"[3]

Regardless of the theories, pastors who intercede learn that few problems will prove impervious to the quiet pressure of secret prayer. As we pray, the Spirit works in hearts and minds out there, bringing conviction to one, softening another, illuminating the mind of yet another concerning some specific conflict or need. The best way for a pastor to control a board or committee is on his knees. He can pray a meeting through before it begins. The best way to handle a cantankerous stubborn member is by prayer (provided it is prayer lifted in love rather than mere exasperation). Prayer can pre-condition moods and atmospheres and thus make the sticky confrontation easier. One pastor of my acquaintance discovered that his Sunday school superintendent and missionary president were having an affair. He prayed with fasting for three days, thus releasing the convicting power of the Spirit upon them, with the result that when he confronted them they were already prepared to listen. Both homes were saved, and the church was spared the devastating calamity of a scandal.

Yes, prayer is work, but it is work that will *work.* It was said of King Uzziah: "As long as he sought the LORD, God gave him success" (2 Chron. 26:5).

Therefore, the pastor who would do God's work in God's way must become a man of prayer. This could prove his most difficult undertaking, for Satan will use every conceivable device, including the pastor's proper duties, to divert and defeat him. He must resolutely elbow his way into the busyness of the day and chisel out time for prevailing prayer.

THE POWER OF PREACHING

Today thousands of people are wistfully turning their eyes to the church. Their interest is cautious, scared, curious, hopeful, tentative. They are strangely both drawn and repelled. Church for many is an unknown venture. But they are disillusioned with the world. They are frightened by what is happening around them. Even more by what is happening to their friends—*and to them.* So they decide to drop into church some Sunday morning. How they are greeted, where they are seated, the music, the atmosphere: all will be a favorable or unfavorable part of their experience. But at some point the pastor will stand up to preach. They will watch him intently and listen carefully. Intuitively they will realize that this is what they have come for. They will not know how to analyze their impressions, but they will sense competence or stumbling. They will feel warmth, sincerity, and genuineness or cold professionalism. They will perceive that he is speaking to their condition or wonder what he is talking about.

If true preaching is happening here, they will find themselves gripped by the unfolding of truth, and sense that at last they have hold of something basic, something elemental, with God at the core of it. And even if they never come back, they will never be the same. They will have been exposed to the power of a sermon and the miracle of it will explode all around them and inside them. They will leave with incalculable and unerasable marks.

At times preachers agonize with a desperate sense of apparent futility. The listeners seem like stone walls. The effects seem so small and so hidden. But let them never fear. When they preach God's truth, articulated by the skill of a careful craftsman, sized and shaped to the needs of the people with loving care, saturated with prayer and delivered with unction, then let the man of God know that the most powerful force in the world is being unleashed. Ideas, truths, pictures, insights are seeping and popping into craniums out there, even the thick ones. "My word," God says through Isaiah, " . . . will not return to me empty, but will accomplish what I desire and achieve the purpose for which I sent it" (Isa. 55:11). The Holy Spirit takes the words of an anointed messenger and as they leave his mouth turns them into lamps, swords, bread, salt, arrows, and balm. And the same word may be a sword for one heart and balm for another. Yes, this happens, when God's Word is preached.

True are the words of the famous surgeon, Dr. Howard Hamlin, spoken to his son-in-law: "There is no higher calling than to preach Christ's gospel!"[4] It is high time therefore that pastors rediscover the glory and power and centrality of preaching. But this will require, in many cases, a radical revamping of time management. Unfortunately the lopsided priorities and pressures of the modern church are not conducive to the mastery of the preaching art or to the depth of study and thought necessary for consistently solid content. Samuel Young says, "A man must go deep into theology if he is to make it simple and yet be sure it is sound."

Because too often pastors come into the pulpit breathless from the week's feverish activity they resort to haranguing. Their people become stultified by week after week of thirty minutes of pathetic attempts at emotional arousement, or by tiresome exhortations to give more and do more, or by repetitious trivialities, or a rehash of the latest ideas from a book which was picked up the night before. But if pastors will come once again to a clear perception of the power of preaching, perhaps they will make the changes in their operating style which will make strong preaching at least possible.

This chapter has stressed some old yet ever new tried-and-true methods of building churches and building people. Some things change, but these methods never lose their effectiveness. They are the methods that will work when thoroughly and consistently and persistently *worked*—praying and preaching. The third leg of the stool, pastoral calling, will be discussed in the next chapter. Naturally these activities need to be buttressed by strong organization. But organization can only provide support for the main lines. It can never substitute for them.

This book is supposed to be about leadership principles. Very well. One of them is that successful application of all the others is this: true leadership begins with depth in the prayer closet and competence in the pulpit.

Pastors, which will it be? Will we do God's work God's way by being men of the Spirit and men of prayer, or will we try to do God's work the secular way?

10

THE MINISTRY OF CALLING

It seems contradictory to be telling pastors to spend more time in their studies and then urge them to spend more time in pastoral calling. But it is still true that a home-going pastor makes a church-going people (Theodore Cuyler). Homer J. Adams says that "if a pastor does not like to visit and avoids this responsibility, he should have his priorities examined." He further adds, "A pastor is in the people business, and there is no way he can handle all his relationships from the pulpit."[1]

Paul found time for both. He testified to the Ephesian elders that he had taught them "publicly, and from house to house" (Acts 20:20, Phillips). And many another great preacher has also been a great caller—including Thomas Chalmers and Phillips Brooks. Even Wesley, itinerant evangelist though he was, found time to visit the poor in their homes. The late Robert G. Lee, pastor of large Baptist churches in Memphis and elsewhere, reported to Leslie Parrott that through most of his ministry he customarily made fifteen calls a day—but now had reduced the number to ten since he was seventy-five years of age! Yet he was a prince of pulpiteers.[2]

THE MAGIC OF THE PASTORAL CALL

It is unfortunate that in the minds of many pastors today pastoral calling went out with the dodo. But the obsolescence is only in the minds of pastors, not the people. Everywhere there is a yearning for the pastor to come in person. People want their needs and problems dignified by the pastor's personal attention, preferably in their homes. Pastoral failure in this matter is a common complaint.

In one case restlessness in a church was so unsettling and ominous that the superintendent suggested to the pastor that he might be wise to move. Accordingly one Sunday morning he announced his resignation. But the board asked for a meeting. It was a two-hour session. The pastor had imagined all sorts of things—that they didn't like his preaching, that they didn't like his leadership, and so on. But he learned to his astonishment that they were really unhappy about only one thing: he did not call. When he humbly promised at least to try to learn, they asked him to rescind his resignation, which he did.

Admittedly pastoral calling is more difficult today, with scattered city parishioners, husband and wife both working, the monopoly of TV in the evenings, and other obstacles thrown up by our fast-moving hectic lifestyle. But still not impossible. Admittedly also more of the one-to-one contacts are in the form of counseling sessions in the pastor's office. But if we think this takes the place of a home call we are in error. In one case I spoke to a pastor about one of his members who was housebound and suffering from an incurable disease. He responded with genuine concern, but explained that just the day before he had had a lengthy counseling session with the wife *in his office*. He was sincerely under the illusion that he had discharged his pastoral duty. Yet when I called a few days later as a friend, the weary wife expressed her grief that during all the long months she had been struggling with her burden, not one member of the ministerial staff had set foot inside the house.

Few pastors seem to have any idea of the sheer magic of a pastoral visit. There is something emotionally satisfying to typical laymen when the man of God shows enough interest to put forth effort to visit in their homes where he can read the Bible and pray and perhaps inquire into their spiritual welfare. This may sound sentimental to blasé moderns, but underneath the crust it is still sentiment which keeps the wheels turning. No amount of involvement in church activities *at the church* can equal pastoral calling as a means of bonding pastor and people. (The nearest thing to it is for laymen to eat at the parsonage table.)

In one pastorate I noticed a family of visitors Sunday morning. In the crush of our small vestibule, as the people exited after church, I was able to catch only the last name and learn that they lived on "River Road"—a several-mile-long meandering semi-rural road. Monday morning I started out, determined to find them. I did, and had prayer with the wife and small children. During our breakfast the next morning the husband, en route to work, knocked at our back door. "I just wanted to thank you," he said. "You are the first pastor who ever prayed in our home." Yes, we got the whole family.

That was just one of the many experiences which convinced me that there is a subtle spiritual force in a pastor's presence in a home which is incalculable. I have never gotten over the wonder and astonishment of it (partly because I never considered myself good at it). But the magic is there. We should capitalize on this magic in sincere, loving ministry to our people.

THE RATIONALE OF CALLING

Pastoral calling can be defined as that form of ministry which is taken by the pastor to the people where they are. It differs from counseling in two ways: The counselee takes the initiative and comes to the pastor, whereas in calling the pastor takes the initiative and goes to the people; also counseling is normally carried out at the church, while pastoral calling is in the homes of the people. Naturally the two overlap, since a call in a home may involve counseling. But still the movement is by the pastor to the people rather than by the people to the pastor.

If defined broadly, pastoral calling includes hospital visitation. But if so, this is a special category which we may designate as crisis care. Strictly speaking, regular pastoral calling is not crisis care—though at times it may prove to be. But pastoral calling is a form of ministry in which the pastor seeks out his sheep for personal attention—to discover how they are doing spiritually, to counsel and encourage (or, rarely, even rebuke), to teach and instruct, at a personal and face-to-face level which is impossible in the public setting.

There are at least six values in pastoral calling:

1. *It is the best way to know one's people* and establish ties of affection and understanding.

2. *It is ideal for reinforcing one's pulpit ministry.* In the informal, relaxed setting of a pastor's visit in the home, members may raise questions about the previous Sunday's sermons which are important to them but which they would not take the initiative to raise otherwise. When what one has preached publicly can be explained and reaffirmed privately, the benefit is double, hence more lasting. Calling thus provides a way of augmenting and confirming one's pulpit work.

3. *It is the best way to discover the people's needs.* This in

turn provides guidance for one's preaching. The members of one church complained that their pastor was busy answering questions no one asked. He and they were not on the same wavelength. He was missing their needs because he did not know what their needs were. Faithful home calling with frank discussions while there would have clued the man in to their thinking and to their problems. The value of his pulpit ministry would have skyrocketed. Preaching that builds is preaching that is relevant to the needs of the people listening.

It is a mistake to suppose that a pastor can glean understanding of his congregation's needs from the counselees who come to his office. He may understand *their* needs but they may not be typical. The majority of his members normally do not seek counseling in a formal setting. Doctrinal, spiritual, ethical, interpersonal problems may nag at them, but not sufficiently for them to take the initiative and set up an office appointment. Their questions and needs must be ferreted out by the initiative of a home-going pastor.

4. *House calling is the best insurance against pew irritability.* People will put up with second-rate preaching longer and more patiently if they love the preacher and feel a bond of love and confidence because he has ministered to them in their homes, face to face and heart to heart. The same is true with "close" preaching. The prophetic-type pastor who holds a high standard and draws sharp lines will not be so likely to provoke knee-jerk hostility if he has built relationships of friendship and confidence. His bonded sheep will sense his true spirit, and perceive him as a loving shepherd who happens to be using the rod.

5. *Finally, home calling is the most effective way to acquire leadership leverage.* This is one of the principles that form the primary subject matter of this book. When a pastor loves his people enough to seek them out on a one-to-one

or family basis and really *minister* to them in that kind of relationship, their willingness to follow his leadership in all the other facets of church life grows exponentially. Home calling will often win alienated members, defuse hostility, and transform foot-dragging into eager marching more effectively than a dozen haranguing sermons.

A timely call may be all it takes to turn a bad tide. In one of my pastorates I became painfully aware that one couple was drifting into a critical, indifferent mood. One Sunday they were absent from both services. After the evening service I drove to their house, knocked at the door, and was let in by two astonished people. I simply said I had missed them, and wondered if they were ill. There was no scolding, only loving inquiry From that moment on they were not only faithful, but almost puppyish in their loyal support and lifelong friendship. They concluded that if the pastor cared enough for them to make a trip after church he wasn't such a washout after all. And the change extended to their three teenage sons, one of whom later became a professor in a holiness college.

OUR ALIBIS—WILL THEY BEAR SCRUTINY?

If pastoral calling is so important, both to the people and to the pastor's own overall ministry, why do so many pastors neglect it? Perhaps some have been infected—as already noted—with the notion that it is outmoded. They had better "disinfect" themselves. Others are just plain scared. They do not know how to make a pastoral call. For a grown man called to the ministry this will not do. Any person who truly loves his people can discipline himself to lay aside his books (or golf clubs!) and get out among them—even if he is tempted, as I was in my first pastorate, to hope that no one would be at home. It is said that Phillips Brooks would often climb the stairs in

Charleston (Boston) to call on the poor, and sometimes just sit in silence. But they knew he was there, that he cared enough about them to come, and they were honored.

The alibis concocted for weasling out of calling are incredible. An evangelist reported to me that in one revival, where he stayed in the parsonage, he called alone every afternoon and preached at night. He finally extracted a promise from the pastor to call with him on Wednesday afternoon at one o'clock. When he opened his bedroom door to go downstairs he was met with a cloud of dust. The pastor, with an apron on, was busy sweeping. He said, without blushing, "You go on, Brother. It isn't fair to leave all the work to my wife. I must stay and help her." No such dust raising had occurred on other days!

My own recall nets the memory of a pastor who was equally derelict. I asked about the occupants of the house next door to the church, directly behind the parsonage. He didn't know. So I called there and found a widow living alone. In the visit I asked if she ever went to the church next door. No, she didn't. I asked why. She said, "No one ever invited me." She was in service that night. Next door to the parsonage, also behind the church but on a different corner, was a young couple with two small children. I urged the pastor all week to ask them to the revival. He never went near. Finally on Saturday I went myself. What made the pastor so overly busy during these days of "revival"? He was repairing the family house trailer, getting it ready to go on vacation early Monday morning!

One pastor's congregation steadily declined. A retired elder said to him, "I notice that Brother X has not been attending recently." "No," was the reply, "he doesn't believe in holiness." The nosy gadfly persisted, "Have you gone to him to talk about it? Have you ever sat down with your Bible and sought to explain the teaching?" The answer was no.

In another case a pastor presided twelve years over a dying church. He went to all the church growth seminars within reach, read all the books, developed graphs of his church's history, and compiled alibis by the dozen— "run-down neighborhood," "wrong location," "people don't like my program," etc. (They really didn't know that he had any.) Meanwhile, he would not call. Not on the neighbors. Not on the members. Not on the prospects. Not on the backsliders. Not on the drifters. When one of his members walked out on his wife (a board member), he never went near. He made no effort to contact the man; no effort to minister to the wife. When he finally moved, the church was only a shadow of what it had been when he became its pastor. Yet he was a good, likable person, and a reasonably good preacher.

Space for such unbelievable anecdotes is justified by the hope that pastors who read these lines will see just how ludicrous their alibis are for not calling. But while ludicrous, their failure is not funny. It is shameful and criminal, for it is a betrayal of trust, and an evasion of their obligations as shepherds of the flock.

Perhaps it is time that we look our excuses for not calling squarely in the face and honestly evaluate them.

WAYS AND MEANS

It must be conceded that pastors of very large churches may be understood if they tend to leave house calling to associates. However, even this excuse can be over-rationalized. Attention has already been called to Robert G. Lee who made fifteen calls a day and then when he reached seventy-five reduced the number to ten. His secret was his concentration and organization. With the help of his assistants, specific categories of need were selected—seriously ill, the bereaved, prospective members, new converts, etc. These calls were organized geographically for minimum time and travel and held to about fifteen minutes (the typical time of a medical office visit). Perhaps not everyone has the stamina for this kind of grueling schedule and still produce great sermons; and indeed in some areas such a brief call would not be acceptable.

There are several types of calls:

1. *The emergency or "crisis care" call.* This is the visit of the pastor because of illness or death. When these needs arise, promptness is essential. The receptivity of the people in need wanes in proportion to the waiting time.

2. *The routine care call.* This is not necessarily a crisis situation, but relates to the chronically ill and aged, those who are perhaps housebound or even bedfast. A mark of a good shepherd is the faithful attention he gives to the sheep who are ill or disabled. This may not be very glamorous to the impatient, ambitious ecclesiastic; but the truth is, in the minds of most laymen there is no more unforgivable failure than for a pastor to neglect the aged and ill.

3. *The incomplete call.* The pastor finds no one at home but leaves his card, perhaps a note, and maybe a tract or magazine. This is not without value. The people know he has at least been thinking of them and put forth the effort to come to their home. However, the sincerity of his effort will be questioned if there is no follow-up.

4. *The social call.* This is a meal in the home or a time of fellowship to which the pastor and his wife have been invited, perhaps after church. While every occasion which brings a pastor into direct contact with his people should be guarded against influence-injuring levity, and while the pastor should always be alert to opportunities for ministering on a spiritual level—right then and there—

these social events are not primarily pastoral in purpose. There will be more lighthearted fellowship and probably jokes and laughter than might be suitable in a formal pastoral call. The pastor will seldom be in error by closing such a time with prayer; on the other hand he does not need to feel bound to turn what is designated as a social event into a preaching service or prayer meeting. Occasionally the Spirit may prompt such a turn, but let it be the Spirit not the pastor's misguided zeal.

5. *The survey call.* This is the "cold-turkey" door-to-door approach, by which the pastor (often with the help of others) surveys a neighborhood. He desires to make himself known to the church neighbors, for one thing. He also seeks an inventory of the religious leanings and needs of the community. Of course the process, properly handled, may yield names of interested persons. The crucial test of the pastor's ingenuity will be the way he implements effective follow-up. Surveys not followed up are worse than no survey at all.

6. *The evangelistic call.* This is a call on a prospect specifically for the purpose of explaining the gospel and leading him to the Lord. It is an ideal form of evangelizing. Was there a visitor in the Sunday services? Was a hand raised for prayer? If possible the pastor is the one who should seek these persons out, the very next day, ideally, or at least during the week. Some of his most fruitful soul-winning efforts will be in the home.

7. *The trouble-shooting call.* This can take many forms because it can concern different types of problems. There is the neglectful church member who needs confrontation. I heard Charles Swindoll say that he had been losing sleep over certain persons who were not living right. He concluded by saying, "I know I am going to have to face them."

Then there is the offended church member who has had a falling-out with others and needs to be counseled and prayed with. The falling-out may be with the pastor himself. If so, this is all the more reason for a prayerful, loving visit. Try to learn the cause of the disaffection, and correct it if possible. Some people enjoy being on the outs and the attention it brings them. But the pastor should not prematurely diagnose this as the case. By tact, patience, loving explanations, and affirmations of love and confidence alienated persons can usually be won back. When they are, they usually become the pastors staunchest supporters. In any case, known disaffection should not be neglected. What is at first a minor problem can, if not promptly antisepticized, quickly become a raging abscess endangering the whole church body.

While "there are issues and matters which take care of themselves if just left for a little while," Richard F. Zanner concludes, he nevertheless cautions pastors, "As a responsible leader, you are called upon to deal with each problem which arises, be it an issue or a person. Deal with it in a responsible, mature and firm, but also very gracious way."[3]

8. *The special-interest call.* Many times pastors need to make calls on their people in their place of business, over a lunch perhaps, or preferably in their homes, in order to present a project. It may be that a board member must be alerted in advance of a forthcoming proposal. Or a reluctant board member who needs, if possible, to be brought around to a supportive attitude. Or the pastor desires to enlist a worker—perhaps to teach Sunday school or serve in some other capacity. Presenting these openings in the person's home will lend credibility and importance to the need far more than an offhand request in the aisle of the church.

9. *The pastoral call.* Of course, every call listed above can properly be called a pastoral call. Yet in the narrower sense we have come now to see that there needs to be a kind of call made for no special reason at all except that

the pastor wants to make pastoral contact with his people. Pastors of large churches may be unable to make many such calls. Let them make each one count. Most pastors, however, can systematically be in every home several times a year if they organize properly.

Methods, of course, must be innovative. One pastor said he made all arrangements in advance by phone. That prepared the people, they were more apt to turn the TV off, were less apt to be embarrassed by a disheveled house, and more psychologically ready for a pleasant yet serious interview. And as for the pastor, he was not wasting time and rubber driving across town to find no one home.

What should the content of such calls be? They should be first of all relaxed and friendly, perhaps with a period of small talk. This should be followed by inquiry into the family's welfare—how Johnny is doing at college or in the army, whether the business has picked up, and any matter which the pastor knows (or should know) to be of special concern. At some point the question of *spiritual* welfare and progress should be quietly raised.[4] The response can determine the direction of the rest of the visit: an appropriate brief passage of Scripture, a brief prayer—or longer if a real prayer meeting needs to be the direction—and a gracious, quick farewell. Don't dawdle at the door. Don't be lengthy. And a reading item left behind is a good investment, as part of the pastoral ministration.

Sometimes pastors have a special theme, coupled with a matching bit of literature, which they plan in advance and try to follow (flexibly) in each home on a particular round of calls.

Pastors can best realize the potential benefits of calling by studying carefully the values listed above and shaping their calling philosophy and methodology with these values in mind. At any rate, here is a neglected dimension of the contemporary pastoral ministry, which in part at least may explain both barrenness and restlessness in many cases. A resolute commitment to tapping the potential of this form of ministry could bring a new day of contentment and effectiveness in the life of many pastors, and certainly a brighter tone into the life of the church.

11

LEADERS LAYMEN LOVE TO FOLLOW

"It is a different world today, and it is far more difficult to be a pastor in today's world than it was as recently as the 1950s," writes Lyle E. Shaller.[1] The baby boomers look at life differently than the previous generations. Technological state-of-the-art changes and rapid developments have made people more concerned with excellence and quality, and this includes not only things such as cars and TVs but functionaries such as pastors. The old-fashioned virtues of dependability and faithfulness are no longer sufficient reasons for churches to put up with a pastor; they demand competence at least comparable to that of other professionals.

Also, the anti-authority mood which gripped much of society in the sixties left its wake in the church, with the consequence that laymen are more reluctant to follow leadership. But as W. E. McCumber says,

> Some of the problems we brought on ourselves. We listened to a few misguided persons who clamored for pastors to become church managers instead of spiritual leaders—a folly the apostles decisively rejected. Now we are victims of the "fire the manager" syndrome that marks unhappy stockholders in corporations whose products can be quantified and whose "bottom line" is fiscal.[2]

In view of this mood it is essential that we have a good handle on the nature of pastoral leadership.

THE SPIRITUAL NATURE
OF PASTORAL LEADERSHIP

Pastoral leadership differs radically from that leadership which rests solely in the inherent authority of an administrative or managerial position. In the secular order, underlings follow the boss because he is just that— in charge. They may disagree with him, even hate and malign him, but they will follow if they want to keep their jobs. This is muscular leadership. But church leadership is light-years removed. The church is an organization which depends for its strength on its nature also as a spiritual organism. Its members are melded into the body by the Spirit, and the body's cohesiveness and efficiency are totally dependent on love, confidence, and voluntary cooperation.

Denominations normally have printed disciplines which are legally binding. These define structures, procedures, and lines of authority. But the real bond of unity is not to be found in these printed disciplines but in the spiritual dynamics which make a church a church. All relationships remain voluntary. No one is required to be a member of a church or to remain in it if he once joins. Therefore his obedience, or "following," cannot be required. It can only be given. It is Christian only as long as it is an offered service rather than exacted. Religious totalitarianism in any form is cultic. As such it is totally foreign to the nature of the Christian faith.

Pastoral leadership therefore is essentially spiritual. This is true in two respects. First, *organizational and administrative leadership cannot be separated from the pastor's primary role as the spiritual leader.* The activities of the church cannot be compartmentalized, with the pastor's role as spiritual leader in one compartment and his role as administrator in another. The pastor's personal spirituality and his spiritual leadership must pervade everything he does, including writing contracts and conducting board meetings. He cannot be pious in the pulpit and a scrooge when handling tradesmen. He cannot be compassionate with the sick and dictatorial and hardfisted when at work in the office.

Everyone who is in touch with the pastor as administrator—his secretary, treasurer, trustees, the outside world—must sense that here, one hundred percent of the time, is a man who is governed in everything he does and every move he makes by the spiritual realities which underlie his calling.

But the pastor's leadership is essentially spiritual in that second respect also, the *invisible bond of love and confidence which makes people willing to follow him.* Certain corollaries follow from this. One is that his official installation as a leader is no assurance of long-range success as a leader. The pastor will succeed only as long as people are willing to follow. Another corollary is that great skill and ability as an *administrator* does not in itself constitute pastoral leadership. Good administrators are often poor leaders.

Since cheerful following cannot be compelled, it can only be won. Yet without cheerful following effective leadership is impossible. All of which means that the pastor's leadership style must be winsome. It must be marked by large amounts of wisdom, tact, diplomacy, consistency, patience, and minimal amounts of whip-cracking. Peter Wagner says, "If a pastor ever has to cajole or beg or threaten a congregation in order to gain leadership, it is a sure indication that he or she does **not** have it and will probably never get it."[3]

SOME MARKS OF A STRONG LEADER

He wants strong people around him

The strong leader seeks to surround himself with the ablest associates possible, both lay and paid staff. Unfortunately, some pastors are afraid of persons who are better educated, more experienced, perhaps more capable than they are. This is not only personal smallness, but it is self-defeating. A pastor should thank God for the top-flight people in the church and use them to the hilt. If he is wise, he will ride to success on their backs. This means enlisting from them their ideas and counsel. It will mean putting them into positions where their special abilities can be utilized to best advantage.

A pastor should see these people not as threats but as members of the team, striving together in a common commitment. It is true maturity when a pastor can respond easily and comfortably with the words, "That's a good idea—let's go for it!" There is something brittle and fragile—and not a little pathetic—about the pastor who feels he must pack his boards and committees with weak people in order to guard his control.

While strong-mindedness may at times seem to impede progress, in the long run the very diversity of views voiced in a board or on a committee will prevent hasty actions and lead to a more balanced and mature consensus. A leader so surrounded may seem to be chained, but in reality he is protected and his long-range program will be stronger. There will be less backtracking to try to undo foolish actions or get out of debacles which were self-created.

A pastor multiplies his talents and energies when he turns strong people loose. Let him encourage them, stand by them when they stumble, honor them publicly (though sanctified workers won't be looking for that), let them know how much the pastor depends on them. The result will be expansion and improved effectiveness everywhere.

The occasional frustration created by lay strong-mindedness may be exacerbated when in addition to being strong these persons are also carnal. As such, they may be motivated by a selfish agenda and controlled by a worldly-minded perspective. They are excessively cost-conscious and materialistic. Let the pastor get extra close to these persons. Love them, listen to them, talk to them—and pray like a house afire! In the meanwhile, gently refuse to allow them to call the shots.

It takes a lot of canny shrewdness to work with a strong person without letting him completely take over. One millionaire board member said to his new pastor, "Come down to the dealer with me. I want to buy you a nice car." The pastor firmly but kindly replied, "No, you won't." When the astonished businessman asked, "Why not?" he replied, "If I let you buy me a new car you'll have me in your pocket." Time proved him right. Yet the relationship was strengthened because the businessman had found his match. It is astonishing how many "sanctified" (and zealous) laymen there are who subconsciously suppose their money entitles them to special power.

But lay leaders who are sanctified through and through, and demonstrate it daily by their unselfish commitment, are worth their weight in gold and should be cherished. Let the pastor capitalize on their expertise. But be equally careful not to burn them out by overloading them.

He shares initiative

Of course most plans will be originated by the pastor. His people expect this much of him. If he has no glowing ideas they will come to wonder what kind of a dud they have on their hands. But at the same time ideas should be a corporate enterprise in source, shaping, and implementation, not a private monopoly. Laymen will think hard about the problems if they know that their ideas will neither be ignored nor routinely shot down.

Furthermore, the pastor should be so personally secure that initial disagreement with his proposals will not unhorse him. All proposals should become the property of the corporate intelligence, no matter with whom they originate, and mulled over in complete freedom and openness. No one should be out to protect his ego at such times. The ego should be given a sedative and put to bed before board meeting.

At times the pastor may have to concede in complete humility that his idea was not such a brilliant one after all. If he is comfortable in his own self-esteem, he will be able to laugh about it but will lose no sleep over it. Nor will he try to cover himself by defense mechanisms. Any loss of face will be solely in his own mind.

The pastor's ideas had better be good most of the time, however, or he will create the image of a bungler. To prevent this, let the pastor avoid snap judgments and impulse proposals. Ideas should be carefully thought through in advance. Let the pastor do his homework and marshal his facts with competence and honesty. Only then will he command the respect of the canny laymen before him. Before presentation it would be well, when the ideas are still tentative, to bounce them off one or two trusted friends. If they are no good, let them die a decent death in discreet silence.

It is a foolish pastor who ramrods a plan through just because it is his and he is obsessed by a proprietary compulsion to put it over. Plans that cannot be a joint venture between a pastor and his board or council should be quietly shelved. If the idea itself is basically sound, it is a weak leader who cannot sell it to his people. This may take time, but the pastor must be patient enough and sufficiently self-disciplined to take time. One successful pastor and denominational leader reported that in his pastorates, if an idea was rebuffed when first presented, he would accept the rebuff cheerfully and courteously, then quietly re-present it a month or two or six months later. Presumably, the second presentation might well be modified to accommodate the opposition, but if he was convinced the project was something they ought to do he did not drop it completely. But neither did he ramrod it through.

Sidney Martin of the famous Parkhead Church in Glasgow operated the same way. He never sought to stampede his board. He respected their opinions and accepted their verdict—for the present. But he kept coming back, gently talking, explaining, praying, until in time he had everyone solidly with him. Could such leadership have been a secret of his more than thirty-year tenure?

The leadership is not only weak but tricky that resorts to a trumped-up case for pushing pet projects through. A sign of this is an attempt to stifle discussion or to brush aside probing questions. It is to be feared that in most such cases some data are being kept out of sight. Trickiness is signaled also when the pastor is so determined to implement his program *now* that he makes an end-run around both his official board and denominational *Discipline* and resorts to extralegal means. He is foolish to suppose that the limb he climbs out on will not be cut off.

When a pastor commits the folly of all follies and, by-passing his board altogether, barnstorms an idea publicly with amateur flair and hype (probably declaring that the plan is straight from heaven) and then is slapped down by his board, he will suffer from well-deserved embarrassment. But more seriously, whatever forward momentum there had been will be stalled, and must be regained by first reestablishing rapport and equilibrium.

He avoids small majorities

John Henry Jowett advised, "Never move with small majorities." Even if by manipulation, high pressure, and fast talking the pastor can manage to squeeze out a bare majority of votes, he will be unwise to proceed. What is legal is not always smart. Why lead half a flock? The opposition of the minority, whether overt or covert, will haunt him from then on. He will have introduced a restive ferment into the body, which may in the end destroy its health and cripple its effectiveness.

When pastors drive through with small majorities they manifest short-term vision. A man of skill will wait until he can lead the whole flock. A keen observer noticed in America a rancher driving a flock of sheep with a pickup, then remembered that in the Holy Land the shepherd led the sheep. He recalled the words of Jesus, "My sheep know my voice, and they follow me." Then he pointedly asked, "Pastor, are you ahead leading or behind driving?"

He respects structures

The very spirituality of the bond between pastor and church makes it all the more important that he respect the structures and processes, and avoid arrogating to himself authority that has not been given him. One young pastor in his first church told me that he found one fair-sized adult class in the Sunday school. "The first thing I did," he said, "was to divide the class." *He* divided the class. This is unilateral action of the most arbitrary kind. The young man thought it was a show of leadership. It was no such thing, but rather a mangling of leadership. Where was his official board or the committee responsible for such matters? Officers who are ignored will soon fade away.

In another case a pastor found, when he took over a strong church, that a large class of adults had been using desks and tables for the purpose of more readily taking notes. The first thing the pastor did was to take the tables out, a move not calculated to win friends and influence people. Such arbitrary actions in the name of "leadership" violate the principle of the spiritual nature of the bond which exists in the church and serve only to alienate the very ones whom we so much desire to follow us. That is not the way to promote a "following" spirit, but rather a mutinous spirit.

And again the question must be asked: Were the proper procedures followed? It needs to be reiterated that a pastor who would build true leadership must work through the structure, not bypass it. Every person in the church who has any official relation to any problem or decision should be respected and worked with, not ignored, and certainly not run over roughshod.

THE WEAKNESS OF AUTOCRATIC LEADERSHIP

As has already been conceded, legally the pastor has certain well-defined authorities and responsibilities. But the wheels of his chariot begin to become mired when his modality shifts from gentle persuasion to autocratic unilateral action.

This is not to say that crises never develop which absolutely demand autocratic unilateral action. On such rare occasions the pastor must show himself forthright, decisive, and courageous—a true tower of strength. But the point is that this should not be his customary mode. People will accept the occasional despotism when they know unusual circumstances have required it.

Men who by nature are vigorous, strong leaders must

by prayer and humility work extra hard to preserve flexibility, lest their leadership harden into a Jim Jones syndrome with disastrous results. These are the pastors who must diligently train themselves to work with the ideas of others, to share authority, and to delegate responsibilities. They will avoid making a show of utilizing the proper boards and committees which is mere window dressing. They will learn that in carrying out projects it is not necessary for them personally to control every detail. They will avoid slipping into the Napoleonic illusion that they are infallible gods to their people.

An inflexible, autocratic leadership may make for a tight ship but a frozen one. Ideas not the pastor's will be routinely stifled. In the words of G. B. Williamson, a pastor "may to such an extent insinuate himself into the management of the church that all thoughtful and self-respecting persons will be dwarfed by the pastor's attitude till they cannot work with him." He adds, "They make nincompoops of everyone."[4] Consequently growth is inhibited. Even if people could work with him, one man cannot control in such detail anything but a small operation.

For the same reason, staff relationships will be strained, for this pastor will keep the reins so tight that staff persons cannot be creative and productive. It is true that the pastor is ultimately responsible and needs to be aware of what is going on and to preserve his place as leader. But as far as possible he needs to open the doors and allow some breathing room. Most of all he must learn to consult his people, seek their ideas, respect their positions, and support them. If they are to support him, he must support them. Let not the church be a one-man show.

STRENGTH THROUGH CONCILIATION

A strong leader knows when to be conciliatory. About some things there should be no compromise. But most issues in church life are not the kind of issues on which the health of the church hangs. W. E. Cox said that he learned to handle church boards as he handled bucking broncos as a young cowboy. "When the board starts to buck, relax. If you stiffen up, they will throw you off."

A pastor should be conciliatory when he discovers that his pressure on his people is becoming more than some of them can bear. This writer once began sending strong letters to his Sunday school teachers, every week urging them to call on absentees. One morning he was met at the church door by the teacher of the junior boys, who with trembling lip and obvious agitation announced that he was resigning then and there. The pastor persuaded him to step over to the parsonage where in quiet conversation the real problem finally surfaced. He worked twenty-five miles away in the shipyards, leaving early and getting home late, bone tired. He could not do, he felt, any more than he was doing. But his extreme emotion came out of a profound psychological sensitivity, dating to his boyhood when he had never been able to please his father. Now he couldn't please his pastor either! The pastor apologized, prayed with him on the spot, and promised that there would be no more letters. Relieved and reassured, the dear man went back to the church and continued to teach. Some years later he and his wife felt called into full-time ministry, sold their home, went to school, were both ordained, and spent the latter years of their lives in home mission work. Think of what could have been lost to Christ and the church if the pastor had stiffened and alienated that man!

A conciliatory spirit is especially timely after an

unfavorable vote. When the young pastor was voted out, the church folk came back that Sunday night with fear and trembling, for their memory was keen of a former pastor, who, in a similar spot, preached three months on such texts as "Touch not mine anointed and do my servants no harm" and "Behold, your house is left unto you desolate." They waited therefore with taut nerves for this pastor's reaction. There was an almost audible sigh of relief when he announced as his text, "O magnify the Lord with me, and let us exalt his name together" (Ps. 34:3, KJV), and insisted that no one should be overly upset by what had happened, for no man was indispensable, only God. He was thinking of the sixty-two young adults he had taken into church membership, and he wanted to tie them to the church. Though many of them were stunned and hurt, the crisis was handled in such a manner that not one was lost.

Sometimes it is wise to back off from too rigorous insistence on a policy which in itself is sound. One pastor created opposition, which registered in a few negative votes, by his dogged insistence and the noise he made in enforcing the rule that only committed tithers could serve on the board. An older minister advised, "By your aggressiveness on this issue you have alienated three families and may lose them. You have to ask yourself—is my rule worth this price? Better back off. Keep the rule but do not try to enforce it inflexibly and openly. Better to keep these families whether under ideal conditions or not." His thought was that down the line, by a revival tide and the spiritual deepening of the affected board members, the problem could solve itself.

J. B. Chapman used to advise that if a problem arose which seemed at the moment to be insoluble, instead of picking at it and keeping the sore inflamed, it would often be better to ignore it for a while, preach the promises, and "get the glory down."

This cannot be done by publicly chastising the people for their spiritual poverty and then by sheer might and awkwardness start jumping around "getting the glory down." Let the pastor get blessed himself by praying his situation through in private. Then ignore the problem in public and stop preaching at it or about it. Exhibit joy, love, confidence, quietness of spirit, and start preaching constructive sermons in a completely different field. Do this until the atmosphere changes, others deepen their prayer life, and the blessing catches fire.

12

THE ART OF MOTIVATING

Infinitely more important than putting across one's program is maintaining respect and confidence. Confidence is a delicate jewel and can be easily marred. It is bound to be marred when the people sense any degree of manipulation or trickiness which does not jibe in their minds with total integrity. When this happens the pastor's leadership is fatally wounded.

THE SNARE OF MANIPULATION

Manipulation can be defined as operating with a hidden agenda. There is in it an element of deception because the reasons advanced for actions are not the true reasons, which are kept out of sight. Reasons given are those which are most apt to disarm opposition and allay suspicion. Candidness is sacrificed for strategy. This is a form of motivating which bites back.

A possible example is the fund-raising promotion that is sold to the church as having primarily a spiritual thrust. The weeks of prayer meetings and lay visitation involved are the softening-up process for the later pledging. The real goal is not revival but money. Of course the pastor hopes for revival as a serendipity, but he is most concerned that the church reach the goal in pledges and is promoting the spiritual as a means to that end. Discerning people see through the ruse, and though they may cooperate, are inwardly uneasy. It would be infinitely better to say, "Folk, we need to raise $100,000 for this project. Let's do it. We will pray and plan and organize and work together to reach our goal." Naturally, the plan will have been worked through the board first so that the leadership base for the project is already in place. But now the real reason for the campaign is up front, and everyone feels at ease. Even the diehard opponents at least know what the score is and that no attempt is being made to hoodwink them.

THE WISE USE OF INCENTIVES

An incentive is a promised reward or pleasure which is sufficiently attractive to prompt response which might not otherwise be given. The promise of profit is the entrepreneur's incentive to work hard. What Christian workers often forget is that all of us need incentives; and we forget that there are different levels of incentives, some low and selfish, others high and noble. The Bible is laced with the presentation of spiritual incentives. "Come to me," Jesus said, "all you who are weary and burdened, and I will give you rest" (Matt. 11:28). The prospect of rest is an incentive for coming to Jesus. Peter urged, "So then, dear friends, since you are looking forward to this, make every effort to be found spotless, blameless and at peace with him" (2 Peter 3:14). Apocalyptic certainties are incentives for holy living. Negative incentives are just as powerful. "For we must all appear before the judgment seat of Christ" (2 Cor. 5:10). The prospect is an incentive to behave.

Holiness attunes the heart to the highest level of incentives, viz., the pure pleasure of pleasing God and doing what is right for right's sake. Such persons do not need the extra motivation of special rewards. On this level also is that maturity of character which finds sufficient incentive in the inner satisfaction of knowing that someone has been helped, a job has been done well, or a duty has been fulfilled.

But ranging downward are many levels of maturity and immaturity, altruism or selfishness. We are compelled to face the blunt truth that most people require incentives for doing what they ought to do, incentives which promise them satisfactions on the fleshly or egoistic level. We expect this in children—so little rewards and contests can be highly useful tools when working with children.

The problem is that many of us have a bit of the child in us and enjoy the fun things. We find within ourselves response to more than one level of incentive. As Christians we want the joy of hearing, "Well done, thou good and faithful servant." This is the supreme incentive which keeps us going when all else fails. But along with it we may enjoy the excitement of, for instance, winning first place in a church subscription contest.

The justification for some utilization of the kind of incentives which contests, athletics, and music or drama events may provide lies in two facts:

First, everyone can be drawn in, the immature as well as the mature, the less spiritual as well as the more spiritual. These activities provide a common ground of participation, thus breaking down barriers and fostering a social blending which in itself is fertile ground for spiritual cross-fertilization. Who has not heard of the youth or man who found the Lord after first being drawn into the basketball team. Finding the Lord was not the first appeal, but playing ball.

Second, such an organized effort, even in the form of a contest, serves to focus attention and harness energies more efficiently than almost any other device. In the process unity, relaxation, and goodwill are promoted. And the job gets done.

At this point it needs to be said firmly that the use of fun things as incentives is not appropriate in some areas of church life. Would we give a prize to the person who won the largest number to Jesus? Would we degrade motivation for soul-winning to this level? Moreover, the use of bizarre antics, such as the pastor standing on his head on the roof in celebration of achieving some goal, which are in reality publicity stunts, suggests muddle-headed judgment, for they tend to make both the church and religion a laughingstock.

BREAKING THE ADDICTION OF SECONDARY MOTIVES

While the wise pastor understands the humanity of his people in these matters, and works with human psychology up to a point, he is nevertheless seeking always to raise the spiritual level of his congregation to the point that the spiritual motives are the real underlying driving forces in his church. There is always a peril lest the carrot stick of food, fun, games, and rewards becomes the rule, and then finally the only device which will spark any enthusiasm at all. At this point the pastor had better start praying and fasting for revival.

Here is an example of relying on secondary motives in areas which should be activated by higher motives. In one church the pastor held up on a Sunday morning a large beautiful picture which he promised to the person who would bring the largest number of new people to the forthcoming revival meeting. One young woman took one look and went to work. She had never shown up for the Thursday night visitation program. If asked she would have doubtless protested her timidity. But with the picture as her goal she wrote, phoned, buttonholed and cajoled, with the result that she brought sixty-two new people. And she won the picture. Several months later, at the next revival, she brought no one. There was no picture. Her love was not strong enough to energize her, but her self-interest was.

When the spiritual level is this low, it is easy for some to become pragmatists and adjust pastoral leadership methods down to this level, resorting to carnal appeals in order to keep things moving. Finally the people become so accustomed to this mode of operating that they lose all sensitivity to the farce going on. But we must remember the example of the Pharisees. While they did not put on contests, their giving, praying, and fasting were with selfish motives. Jesus said, "They have received their reward in full" (Matt. 6:2). It would be tragic if Jesus should have to say to any of our churches, "You have pictures and prizes and certificates and name plates and banquets—you are paid in full!"

There is a fine but crucial line between appropriate recognition being given to spiritual people who have worked selflessly for the Lord, and the methodology which relies on manipulative tactics to get a little work out of a lazy flock.

Is there any way to break this addiction? Let the pastor begin with himself. If a man can emancipate himself on his knees from dependency on secondary motives he will be more apt, in time, to transform his church.

Which are the primary motives? Genuine love for God and genuine love for people. This is it—pure and simple. But the love must be deep enough and dynamic enough to prompt everything that secondary incentives can induce—*and then some*. Any rewards and fun things will be incidental, not motivational. The preacher whose love is deepest and purest will be the hardest worker, all for Jesus' sake. And in the long run his work will be the most effective and the most lasting.

CYCLES OF LAY RESPONSE

A frequently missed aspect of the art of motivation is the psychology of cycles of response in our laymen. A pastor who understands this principle and gears into it will be the more successful motivator in the end.

A pastor reported, "My first year and a half in my present church everyone seemed to get behind the chariot and push with enthusiasm and commitment in every department. But the last year and a half the wheels have dragged. My people attend, but the enthusiasm has waned. It is as if they decided within themselves that they didn't really want to be *that* committed." I replied, "Your experience is typical. The probabilities are that in your fourth and fifth years you will see a resurgence of participation and productivity."

I went on to explain: "Often a church will take hold with verve under a new pastor, for there is a certain excitement and impetus sparked by new leadership. But this kind of impetus is rarely sustained. In many cases the pastor, in his intemperate fervor, keeps building up the pressure until a point is reached when it is more than the people can handle. Then they begin to feel frustrated. They sense that they are overextending themselves and quite naturally begin to retrench. This may not be due to spiritual declension but entirely to a discovery of physical and emotional limitations. Lifestyle has become too cluttered and unbalanced, and the imbalance needs to be corrected."

Whether or not this retrenchment becomes a serious spiritual drift depends in large measure on the pastor's skill in handling the syndrome. If, like the green young King Rehoboam (2 Chron. 10), he cracks the whip and turns the screws a little tighter, he may lose some of his top workers. This is not the time to preach strident sermons on consecration and sacrifice, in the process adding a load of guilt to the burden of fatigue. Rather, the pastor needs to understand what is happening, and change both his pace and his tactics. Let him slow down with his people. This is the time to assure them of understanding and full support—without overdoing the matter with paternalistic soft soap.

When the down cycle takes over, the pastor may have to help his people unload some jobs. If he is too slow, they may go to the extreme of rashly resigning from everything. Yet in the process of recognizing the need for restructuring the pastor must walk the tightrope of tact, lest he give the impression that he is too willing to make changes because in his mind they have failed. Affirmation and appreciation must be generous and sincere, together with a vocalized understanding of their need to lighten the load. If the pastor prays with them and urges them to pray alone for guidance, they are more apt to make a spiritually motivated decision than one dictated by jaded emotions and spent energies.

This may mean finding new people for the jobs. In turn this may require putting some folk in whose qualifications are less than ideal. Or it may mean letting some jobs go unfilled. Many churches have multiplied activities until they are top-heavy. The activities exceed their capacity. The church wears itself out turning the wheels. Therefore scaling down the activities is not necessarily a backward step. It could be a rediscovery of essentials and a realignment for the next growth surge.

Pastors too often forget that laymen are human too. They live under heavy demands and pressures in the form of family, vocations, financial burdens, school demands in some cases, plus just plain physical finiteness. Many of them have chronic health problems which limit their energies. No matter how spiritual they are at heart, and no matter how much they want to see the church prosper, they cannot give to the church so much time and energy as some pastors seem to expect.

If the pastor will respect the normal ebb and flow of the human psyche, and love and reinforce his people during the ebb tides, the probabilities are that when they have caught their breath they will take hold again with fresh vigor. The second-time-around enthusiasm will not be the euphoria of new leadership, but the more mature involvement prompted by simple love of the Lord. Moreover, it will be easier now, for they have adjusted to their pastor's style and are not under a tension to please him. Besides, they will feel grateful to him for being their loving shepherd during their personal low tide.

This cyclic principle in church life should also inform the pastor in his programing of special periods of thrust. Generally these intense campaigns come in the fall and in the spring. They may include special prayer meetings, perhaps daily sessions at the church. They may include highly organized outreach programs. But these all-out involvements should have clearly specified terminal dates. Many folk can manage extra effort in prayer or calling for six weeks who would not be able to keep up such an accelerated pace the entire year or even for six months. It is not wise, therefore, for the pastor simply to add a prayer meeting or any such extra load on an indefinite basis, without asking himself whether he can reasonably expect his people to absorb the added activity into their already tight schedules. When a new highly pressurized undertaking is added to the church calendar on an open-ended basis, people bravely try to keep up as long as they can. Then when they begin to drop out they feel guilty. This unfair guilt trip can be avoided by planning time-controlled bulges of overload so that when the time is up everyone can drop back and everyone can feel good about it. The probabilities are that the special drive will leave permanent dividends in the life of the church. Then four to six months later everyone will be primed for a new surge of special effort.

13

OUR PROGRAM—BALANCED OR BLENDED?

Instead of thinking of a balanced church program, we should think in terms of a blended program. If balance alone is our aim, we will try to walk a tightrope between social events and spiritual events, or athletics versus revival. A fatal dichotomy will develop. The social activities will gradually come to be the tail that wags the dog, and the spiritual will get short shrift. It is better to think not in terms of balance but of blending. What cannot be saturated with spiritual meaning and purpose should be resolutely jettisoned.

This blending most fundamentally is that of the human and the divine. Perhaps we can say the hype and the holy. A church succeeding is a church with lots of excitement. Much is going on involving all ages and classes. But somehow the activities must revolve around a spiritual center. If there is laughter and clapping (as in some places), it must somehow be impregnated with spiritual currents by which the thoughts are continually being directed toward Christ. The big musical production for instance, requiring weeks of work, may be no more than a splashy production; or it may be a conveyer of profound spiritual power.

FOSTERING THE IDEAL

How can a church foster and maintain this blending of the human and the divine? Four ways:

First, the leaders need to recognize that the human side of the program attracts outsiders, and is often the first point of contact with the unregenerate. They are not yet spiritually alive but are socially responsive and open to religious activities and ideas.

Second, the quality of everything designed to draw people in must be appropriate to the main objective—the glory of God. Some cheap claptrap will be ruled out. Everything done, even a Hallowe'en party, should be conducted in such a way that the Holy Spirit, instead of being grieved, can work through it. Nothing should ever be done which would disgust thoughtful people who have begun to look up to this church for possible spiritual guidance. This means that whatever cannot smoothly, without stark incongruity, lead into a time of prayer or spiritual talk or a few testimonies, will siphon off power rather than channel it.

The truth here is that the kinds of activities in the church dare not be compartmentalized into spiritual and nonspiritual categories (or perhaps secular and sacred, social and religious). If the athletics, the day care center, the skating parties, the lay retreats, the outings, cannot be sanctified by Christ's presence, if they are not fit subjects for prayer, and if they cannot serve spiritual purposes, then they are offenses in the church and are odious to God. They distract time and energy and obstruct the ministry of the Spirit. They become fatty occlusions in the arteries of the church body and only death can result.

But third, even if activities are inherently capable of serving the true purpose of the church, they will not do so unless undergirded with much prayer. If in the background the praying saints are interceding, if prayer meetings are numerous, if the leaders of the music and youth and social events are also in the prayer meetings, the hype will be holy and edifying as well as exciting. It is incongruous if in the prayer meetings the leaders are conspicuous by their absence.

Fourth, and perhaps most crucial, the leaders must be Spirit-filled men and women. The Apostles demanded this much even of social welfare workers (Acts 6:1–6). This goes for the staff ministers and also for the lay leaders. Their spiritual objectives must be deep and must be up-front. They can promote some bang-up things, but the presence or absence of the Spirit in their own personalities will come through loud and clear. It is this sense of genuineness for which even young people hunger, and which will result in a growing church.

In the prescribed qualifications for deacons, not only was Spirit-fullness named, but good reputation and wisdom (Acts 6:3). No person should be in charge of youth groups, choirs, Sunday school classes, or ushering, who is not respected in the community as a good bill-paying and law-abiding citizen. But neither should a person be in a leadership position who has zeal without sense. The fervency of the Spirit-filled must be combined with the discernment of the wise. This is that ability to weed out the inappropriate activities which are always being suggested by immature persons, and to have the good sense to know propriety in distinction from impropriety. It is amazing how many people have good religion with nary an ounce of judgment. Of course if they were mature enough to know how to discern the mind of the Spirit they would be saved by His restraints and promptings even if they lacked common sense themselves. It is because of these very grave variables that pastors are compelled to keep a sharp eye open and a gentle hand on operations, even when they are trying hard to give some freedom of personal style and initiative.

BLENDING DEPUTATION AND SUPERVISION

A fine blending must be sought in leadership methods also. This includes a melding of deputation and supervision, for one thing. On the one hand is the autocratic leader who either does everything himself or at least makes all the decisions. On the other hand is the laid-back delegator who organizes folk and then plays golf. He assumes that each person will do his or her job without any supervision. In most cases this is an unrealistic expectation. A plant foreman might as well point to a welding machine and say, "Go to work." If he is talking to a welder, fine; but if to a novice, no. Any beginner must be trained. He must be shown what to do and how to do it, and some one near at hand must keep an eye on his production.

This is equally true in the church. Even established Christians often flounder in church jobs which they have never done before. But to turn a new convert loose with a strange church job is to qualify for the top prize in Church Follies. The pastor or his close associates should show the new worker what is to be done and how to do it, then proceed to work with him. The assistance must be tactful and discreet but always near at hand. Whoever is supervising—whether the task is counting money or keeping records or ushering or welcoming visitors or cleaning the church or running a calling program—must keep close to the newly elected or newly appointed worker. First, bring him in gradually so that he works with or under more experienced personnel. Then give more specific training if the job requires it, e.g., suggesting books to be read, classes to be attended, etc. Follow-up is equally important. "How are you getting along? Any problems? Did you find that book helpful?"

"One-Minute Management" works in the church as well as in business. The pastor or his responsible associate should frequently express quietly a word of commendation, then if needed slip in a suggestion. A public word of commendation may prepare the way for the private steering session the following week. The need for in-flight correction is common and is to be expected, but it can be done without embarrassing the worker or causing loss of face. Corrections should reconfirm him as the right person for the job, and reconfirm his self-confidence rather than shatter his confidence and make him feel like a failure. Of course in very extreme cases a change of jobs becomes absolutely unavoidable. But even that can be managed without destroying the person.

A primary principle in church management is *every person who has any job whatsoever must be accountable to someone*. Otherwise there will be a lot of loose cannons around. A few independent actors who do as they please can tear up the works in a hurry. Frequently new church members do not understand that there is a structure which they are to work through. Like it or not, there is a chain of command in the church. Sunday school teachers don't simply hand their classes over to their own chosen successors. Choir members don't recruit their outside friends to sing in the choir without saying a word to the director. This was done once in a certain church and the choir found in their midst one Sunday morning a tobacco-soaked, liquor-drinking unconverted young man whose lifestyle was anything but religious. Tactfully and prayerfully the well-meaning aggressiveness of the inviter had to be handled, fortunately without losing the prospect who was converted in the next revival in spite of having been removed from the choir. In the end he became an ordained elder. Instead of becoming angry, he respected the church's position; in the meanwhile the eager beaver learned a lesson. Our zeal does not license us to be a law unto ourselves in church affairs. Peter says we are to supply our zeal ("virtue") with knowledge (2 Peter 1:5).

Some responsibilities in the church require periodic reporting and evaluation procedures. These procedures may include meetings of the respective committees or councils. Others *warrant* such regular recharging and evaluating sessions even if the regular structure of the church does not prescribe them.

In one of my pastorates I was fortunate enough to have a wise and skillful director of Christian education. She gathered around her once a month her corps of teachers. During that evening she went over with them the lessons for the following month, introduced visual and manual aids, inspired them with enthusiastic pep talks, discussed understandingly their problems, helped them find solutions, and prayed with them. The evening was so fun-filled and love-directed, so permeated with devotion to Christ, that the teachers were always infused with new enthusiasm and dedication. The result was a Sunday school in which teacher tardiness or absenteeism was virtually nil, the pedagogical quality of the school equaled any public school, and children cried when they were prevented from attending.

Here was a corps of willing workers who needed the reinforcing of a skilled leader. And the maturity and wisdom of the leader was such that the pastor's supervision of her was not needed. Fortunate pastor!

TRAINING NEW MEMBERS

In the incorporation of the new members into the functional life of the church two problems are common. One is immaturity with its corollary—lack of discipline. These persons tend to live by meteoric enthusiasm. They are great starters but poor finishers. They become bored quickly and discouraged easily. With these people extraordinary patience is required. We should not be surprised if they take on a job with gusto, only to be absent the next committee meeting. What should be ascertained is whether they truly love the Lord and want to serve Him. If so, the pastor must find ways to keep them on the track. He may fail, but perhaps instead he will succeed, and gradually they will become reliable and efficient workers. If they blow it the first time, give them another job and then another; be very slow to write them off. Keep hoping that some maturing will take place over a period of time. The patience of the pastor and other leaders may contribute to the maturation process. If possible keep them involved *in something* rather than allowing them to sit on the sidelines, feeling unimportant and unwanted.

The other problem confronting the pastor who would incorporate new people usefully is the inconstancy of immaturity compounded by carnality. Handling self-centered babyishness is far more difficult than simple immaturity. These people jockey for position, are envious of the jobs of others, have feelers sticking out all over the place for favoritism, and react chronically to imaginary slights and grievances. Consequently they require frequent coddling. While we must refuse to allow them to monopolize our time and energies, we must at the same time refuse to allow ourselves to cast them off with an impatient spirit. Pastors should double their prayer for these people, and pray for an extra portion of divine love. Many of them have a low self-image behind a pugnacious exterior, they feel guilty, they are hungry for something better, and they hope the preacher will keep on loving them. They may be like the school boy whose meanness is a secret cry for attention. At any rate there is a cure: entire sanctification. So a holiness church offers them more hope than any other kind of church. And a holiness church will put up with them with more grace.

A facet of carnality even more difficult to handle than touchiness is insubordination. A carnal tendency is aversion to leadership and authority. The church structure is resented. The rules are flouted, not just ethical rules but polity regulations. To cap it all off these persons often resist leadership in the name of private guidance, with the gauntlet, "I will obey God but not man." A form of this is the grandiose talk about freedom in the Spirit, which in their view is stultified by church rules and regulations. "A spirit of independence is the essence of carnality." Holiness of heart and lowliness are twins. The sanctified person can work under rule and can work under leadership.

For the last several chapters we have been discussing some basic leadership principles. Much more could, and perhaps should, be said. But for now let us summarize the basic, indispensable qualities of personal character and leadership style a pastor must display if his people are going to follow gladly. Whatever specific methodology he may adopt, its lasting success will depend on the spirit which underlies his methods.

The people will follow if they sense in their pastor (1) essential goodness, (2) authentic competence, (3) a spirit of service rather than a lust for position and power (1 Peter 5:1–4), (4) a willingness to work, (5) a teachable spirit, and (6) basic soundness of judgment. If all of this is in place and becomes increasingly apparent, the sanctified people—and all of goodwill—will follow him with gladness. A sense of security will bond church and pastor into an unbreakable force for God.[1]

14

THE LOSS AND RECOVERY OF SELF-ESTEEM

This chapter may seem to be an anticlimax. But it could very well prove to be an open sesame to a new beginning. It will take courage, humility, and honesty to make a rigorous application of this chapter to oneself.

First, let us review the "borderline" situation (chapter 6). There are many pastors who aren't quite making it, and won't if present trends continue. Others are just barely making it, enough to stay in the ministry, but moving too frequently from one church to another, until they finally wearily reach retirement.

I once heard J. B. Chapman tell preachers that being right forty-nine percent of the time would spell net failure, while being right fifty-one percent of the time would mean success. Failure/success hanging by a hair! But who wants to make it by a hair? If our ambition is sanctified, fifty-one percent provides little satisfaction.

So there is a third group. These men and women are considerably beyond fifty-one percent but are still falling far short of their potential. Deep in their hearts they know it, and the people sense it too, though they may not know how to put their finger on the problem.

It is too easy for these pastors to think that radical changes are needed in the people or in their location.

They should face up to the possibility that the radical changes may need to occur in them. It has already been observed that so often the problem consists of a complex of small, gnawing faults which could be corrected. But how is a person going to correct weaknesses he does not see? The first task therefore is diagnosis. This is why profiting by this chapter will require humility, courage, and honesty.

Most of us could be more effective as pastors and ministers of the gospel than we are. Steady improvement should be our aim. But there are special crises, difficult turning points, and painful life changes which demand profound remaking of the preacher as a person. If these recastings do not occur, the man or woman very likely will drift out of the ministry, perhaps defeated and embittered. But if the person is willing to be changed he will emerge on a higher plane of usefulness. There will be a new dimension to the man's soul and to his spiritual power, a revitalized commitment, and probably a greatly lengthened ministerial tenure. Someone has said, "God will pull us through if we are willing to stand the pull."

THE TRAUMA OF CRITICISM

The greatest obstacle to this kind of ministerial overhaul is the ego barrier. For the kinds of change most needed are those which strike at the core of self-esteem. Some of us need literally to be taken apart and put together again. But this cannot be done without submitting ourselves to the process. And it requires the hardest thing any preacher can do: look at himself objectively and intelligently. But no matter how hard he tries thus to look at himself, it will be almost impossible for him really to see himself as others see him. If he attempts to do the job on his own, he is still protecting his ego. The new self-image which emerges may be as distorted as the old one.

There is no substitute for the rawhide of criticism even though we wince and dodge under the blows. We should invite it from our superintendent, wife, children, neutral professionals, and even our own board or council members. Preachers mistakenly think that if they open themselves to the candor of church members they will lose their leadership. The precise opposite is more likely to be the case.

What if we are ripped open by unqualified, ignorant people who are perhaps carnal and mean in addition? Well, what they say to us they have probably said a hundred times behind our back. Isn't it better to know what they are thinking and saying? Even if their spirit is wrong, even if they are mistaken in their opinions, we can learn something from them which will make us better persons and perhaps better pastors. "Better is a poor but wise youth than an old but foolish king [pastor], who no longer knows how to take warning" (Eccl. 4:13).

A wise, careful layman approached his pastor with the suggestion—gently made—that he call on a certain family that had a critical need. Stiffening, the pastor replied, "I know how to run this church. I don't need your help." I have seen this sort of rigidity on the part of pastors so often over the years that I am forced to the conclusion that the Achilles heel of the ministry is our inability to handle opposition and to accept criticism or even suggestions. This is tragic because we lose the respect of our best people. In addition, our ministry will remain stagnant. Most men who gradually drift to dead center could be helped out of their trap if they were big enough and childlike enough to grasp the extended hands of competent laymen who could help and are so lovingly eager to do so.

Why this tragic roadblock? In many cases genuine sanctification will remake a pastor's attitudes and bring him down from his high horse. But a very human dynamic is working here which, at least to begin with, may not necessarily be carnal.

In many ways a pastor's ego touchiness is analogous to that of a young husband. He enters marriage under the illusion of husbandly perfection. Fostered by the admiring and adoring worship of his young bride, he perceives himself to be the answer to a maiden's prayer—kind, thoughtful, unselfish, strong, and wise. His continued happiness becomes helplessly dependent on this self-perception. When therefore his wife begins to be critical, his dreamworld collapses. Every argument, every instance of nagging, every sign of wifely disillusionment is a blow to his ego and hence a blow to his self-esteem. He may adjust to reality and regain his balance and allow good sense to stabilize him after the inflated balloon is burst, but the process will be excruciatingly painful. The dreamworld will be gone forever.

Something like this happens to a pastor when the honeymoon is over, the euphoria is past, and the people stop looking up to him with awe in their eyes. At first everyone looks to him for the answer to all things. He is up front. He does the preaching. He plans the services. He presides over business meetings. He delegates responsibilities. Everywhere he turns people ask him, "Pastor, who do you think should teach this class?" "What is your opinion of our Sunday school literature?" "Did you like the choir number this morning?" And so on and on until quite naturally he comes to feel this is the way it should be and always will be. But when the winds of criticism and foot-dragging and negative votes begin to blow, he is shocked, hurt, and puzzled. He feels deserted, alone, helpless, suddenly shorn of his power. Not only is his human ego battered but his professional self-confidence is shaken. He sees his leadership disintegrating.

Actually reality is replacing the mirage. That which will determine the preservation of his leadership will be the maturity and poise his people see in his handling of the opposition and setbacks. And it depends also on the humility and intelligence displayed in the realistic appraisal of his own faults and limitations. The typical congregation does not demand perfection. But members want to work with their leader, not against him, and rigidity on his part makes working with him impossible.

Some men cannot seem to face reality when they are knocked off their pedestal. Their insecurity breeds fear which in turns breeds stiffness. If they can break through this and come out wiser, quieter, more understanding of both themselves and their people, relaxed, accepting their weaknesses as well as their strengths, having forged a new bridge of communication, they will find themselves on a new plateau of personal maturity. Furthermore, they will bring into the church family a new atmosphere of love and confidence and begin to enjoy a greatly enhanced degree of respect from their people. When we allow ourselves to be broken we will be put back together by God Himself into a much better person. Our self-esteem will be healthier, for it will no longer be the child of an illusion.

Such a re-made man or woman who has reached this new level of maturity will come to understand that a no vote is not necessarily an expression of dislike or of insurmountable rejection. Opposition could be right instead of wrong. Someway the pastor needs to achieve such an inner sense of strength and security that he can handle the rough-and-tumble of the pastorate without the loss of self-confidence and self-esteem. He needs to be capable of admitting his humanity and fallibility, and be able to say to his people as well as to himself, "Perhaps I have been wrong"—and say it without emotional collapse.

ACCEPTING ONE'S NICHE

One of the magnificent victories of soul which lie within the reach of every pastor is the victory of accepting one's ecclesiastical level. Every church needs a pastor. Most churches are small; therefore, most pastors will be pastoring small churches. Their best hope of serving a larger church is to make the present one larger.

Furthermore, many men are peculiarly gifted in pastoring the smaller church and would be misfits in larger ones. Can a man be big enough to see this as one of the facts of life and accept it? Or will he allow it to gnaw on him like a carnivorous rat? Can he face his special type of ministry, his own strengths and limitations, with honest realism, and be content to face the fact that the probabilities are that he will spend his life in small churches? These men, who can thus adjust to reality, are the truly noble men. These are the great heroes of the faith.

And can a man be big enough to keep sweet-spirited and hardworking in the face of life's inequities? Or, more especially, ecclesiastical inequities? It is painfully obvious that the best preachers are not always in the "best" churches. The most able administrators are not always elected to the office where their abilities could most fully be realized.

A fact of life for the preacher is that there are several echelons of position and responsibility: the top echelon, then ranging beneath are several lower echelons. At the top (in the very nature of the case), the positions to be filled are always few. *But there may be five times as many preachers perfectly capable of filling those positions as there are needs.* Suppose there are two positions at the so-called top (as Paul says, I speak in human terms), but ten men are capable of filling them. Since there are only two openings, only two of the ten will be called by God and the church to fill them. The other eight will serve on a level below their capacities. What will they do? Kick the traces and sell real estate? Complain about unfairness in selection? Move to another district or conference where they can perchance be a bigger duck in a smaller pond? Or to a conference where the superintendent is old and about to retire? Change denominations and hope for opportunity to match their genius? Or will they cheerfully work at the lower echelon with as much commitment and enthusiasm as they think they would if they were at the higher level? There is no more accurate test of character than this.

It is in these crises and tests that men prove whether they are driven by ecclesiastical ambition or simple love for Christ and souls. If love constrains them, as it did Paul, they will count it a high honor to represent Jesus and preach His gospel in any church, large or small, and will put into it all they have.

R. T. Williams, Sr., when a denominational general superintendent, once said, "The hardest preachers to deal with are those with disappointed ambition." But if holiness doctrine has any validity at all, we are compelled to add that such preachers are the neediest.

PETER'S LESSON

Sometimes the loss and recovery of self-esteem turns not so much on the trauma of criticism as on the collapse of self-confidence respecting acquired and proved skills. When Peter said after the Resurrection, "I'm going fishing," it was as if he were grasping *in the flesh* for the recovery of his self-confidence.[1] He could have been saying, "I may not be much success as a disciple, but I can sure fish! I am on top there! That is one thing I really know how to do!" But he toiled all the night and caught nothing until he once again came under the Lord's rod, and did it—yes, even fishing—the Lord's way.

Jesus was teaching Peter that apart from Him he could do *nothing*. When we start out to serve the Lord, we must put on the altar our know-how—those skills which we are most sure of. For now, in Christ's kingdom everything operates on a different plane, and must be done on the right side of the ship or our nets will be empty. The things which we always could do so well before do not work now. Men have prided themselves on their speaking ability, only to be compelled by Christ to learn all over again. They have entered the ministry with broad business and leadership experience, only to discover that the old ways do not work in this new kingdom. They have directed men in the military or in corporations, but soon learn that their management styles must be radically altered, even to the tone of their voices.

GOADED BY A LETTER

Denis Applebee tells of a crisis in his life when unexpected criticism threatened to overwhelm him. He and his young wife were in their first pastorate. They were both discouraged and decided to go away on a little vacation. When packed and ready to go, they waited for the mail, hoping that perhaps some kind soul would enclose a gift sufficient to help them with their expenses. Instead of money was a letter from the principal of the Bible training school from which Denis had recently graduated.

The letter contained three criticisms. First, the principal wrote, was Denis' habit of tardiness, always with a tidy excuse. Second was his habit of saying, "I forgot," when an assigned task had not been done. Third, was his poor spelling. These faults, affirmed the letter, hurt an otherwise good testimony.

Understandably, the young couple, already discouraged, were now knocked flat. But in that painful moment the young pastor looked up and saw the words of a motto on the wall, "I am thy light and thy salvation." They both seized upon it. The Lord was the light which disclosed through the principal these faults of character. But also the Lord would save from them. On the spot Denis, with his wife's support, resolved to accept the letter as from the Lord and remedy the flaws. Dr. Applebee made the personal comment to this writer, "In the years of teaching, writing, and editing since then, I have had much cause for gratitude for the faithfulness of that kind friend who courageously startled me into facing reality, and challenged me to act."

This was a crucial moment in the young pastor's life. A bad reaction to the letter could have frustrated any possible benefit. Worse, it could have sown in his heart the seed of bitterness which might ultimately have destroyed his ministry altogether. But reactions are choices we make. He and his wife chose to make the letter a steppingstone to improvement, for Jesus' sake and with God's grace. It really wasn't the letter which made him the man he became. That was only the occasion. It was his choice of reaction.

NOTES

CHAPTER ONE

[1]Quoted by James D. Newton in *Uncommon Friends* (New York: Harcourt Brace Jovanovich, Publishers, 1987), p. 100.
[2]C. Peter Wagner, *Leading Your Church to Growth* (Ventura, Calif.: Regal Books, 1984), p. 17.
[3]Ibid., p. 18.
[4]Lyle E. Schaller, *Looking In the Mirror* (Nashville: Abingdon Press, 1984), p. 17.

CHAPTER TWO

[1]Obviously this concentrated focus involves some overlap with previous and subsequent chapters.
[2]Newton, *Uncommon Friends*, p. 288.
[3]In Orlando, Florida *Sentinel;* quoted in *Reader's Digest*, August 1988, p. 130.

CHAPTER THREE

[1]Samuel M. Shoemaker, *With the Holy Spirit and With Fire*, (Waco, Tex.: Word Books, Publisher, 1960), p. 53.
[2]Ibid., pp. 42–43.
[3]*The Seminary Tower*, Fall 1987, p. 5. Dr. McKenna's reference is to Lloyd John Ogilvie, *The Other Jesus* (Waco, Tex.: Word Books, 1986), 75f.

CHAPTER FOUR

[1]*Fellowship Communications* (tape), Prison Fellowship Staff Conference, 1988, Washington, D.C.
[2]Stephen F. Olford, "The Leadership of Christ," in *Giving God the Glory*, ed. by David Porter (Bromley, Kent, England: STL Books, 1985). Quoted in *Decision*, September 1988, p. 26.
[3]While total family involvement is conducive to deepening interest and commitment by parsonage children, it cannot assure such results. Children can be shaped and molded up to a point, but in spite of ideal parental management they, as free moral agents, may rebel and choose the world. When this happens parsonage parents are hurt and puzzled, and feel betrayed. But they should not

emotionally flog themselves, for they and their methods are not necessarily to blame.

CHAPTER FIVE

[1] Lyle E. Schaller, *It's a Different World* (Nashville: Abingdon Press, 1987), p. 123.

[2] Some other titles are *Looking in the Mirror* (Nashville: Abingdon Press, 1984) and *Survival Tactics In the Parish* (Nashville: Abingdon Press, 1977).

[3] William A. Quayle, *The Pastor-Preacher* (New York: The Methodist Book Concern, 1915), p. 143.

[4] Former general superintendent, Church of the Nazarene.

CHAPTER SIX

[1] Late general superintendent of the Church of the Nazarene.

[2] *The Pastor-Preacher*, p. 102.

[3] Currently president of Northwest Nazarene College, Nampa, Idaho.

CHAPTER SEVEN

[1] James D. Glasse, *Putting It Together in the Parish* (Nashville: Abingdon Press, 1972), p. 23.

[2] Quoted from a personal letter to this writer.

[3] *Putting It Together*, p. 63.

CHAPTER EIGHT

[1] Helmut Gollwitzer, *The Demands of Freedom* (New York: Harper and Row, 1965), p. 71.

[2] Of course most laymen do not "love a good fight" and will lean over backward to cooperate, even when they secretly doubt their pastor's wisdom. The worst thing that can develop is a perception in the mind of the pastor that the church council or board is the enemy.

CHAPTER NINE

[1] Erwin W. Lutzer, *Failure: The Back Door to Success* (Chicago: Moody Press, rev., 1976), p. 25.

[2] No vendetta is implied against seminars. Many of them are useful. But they become illusory when they become substitutes for the pastor's own hard thinking and praying for divine guidance. Gary Henecke goes so far as to say, "We want 'how to' seminars because we are working in the energy of the flesh."

[3] *Works* (Kansas City, Mo.: Nazarene Publishing House, reprint of 1872 edition), Vol. 13, p. 32. As evidence Wesley cites Job 42:8; 1 Thessalonians 5:25; and James 5:14–16. For further study of the theology of intercession see the two articles on the subject in *Beacon Dictionary of Theology* (Kansas City, Mo.: Beacon Hill Press of Kansas City, 1983), pp. 288–289.

[4] Dallas D. Mucci, "This Pair of Hands": *Howard Hamlin, M.D.—Man with a Mission* (Kansas City, Mo.: Beacon Hill Press of Kansas City), p. 92.

CHAPTER TEN

[1] *The Preacher's Magazine*, Vol. 59, No. 2 (December, January, February, 1983–84), p. 41.

[2] Admittedly, the very size of his churches provided a strong support system for the organizing of his calling. Nevertheless, *he* made the calls and *he* prepared the sermons.

[3] Richard F. Zanner, Editorial in *Trans-African*, March 1988, p. 8.

[4] I once had in my congregation a sophisticated, urbane man whose spiritual life was very rocky and who astonished me by saying, "I resent the preacher who talks to me about everything but my soul. I appreciate it when someone says to me, 'How are you doing spiritually?' " It was a lesson to me. People know what pastors are supposed to be about, and people are sometimes more concerned about their own spiritual state than appears on the surface. Pastors should not be intimidated by a debonair manner.

CHAPTER ELEVEN

[1] Lyle E. Schaller, *It's a Different World*.

[2] W. E. McCumber, *Herald of Holiness*, September 15, 1987, p. 16.

[3] C. Peter Wagner, *Leading Your Church to Growth*, p. 111.

[4] Gideon B. Williamson, *Overseers of the Flock* (Kansas City, Mo.: Beacon Hill Press of Kansas City), p. 172.

CHAPTER THIRTEEN

[1] According to the American Management Association the four components of management are planning, organizing, leading, and controlling. Obviously these components are as essential to good church management as to a secular business.

CHAPTER FOURTEEN

[1] Suggested in a sermon preached by Denis Applebee.

FOR FURTHER READING

Adams, Jay E. *Shepherding God's Flock: A Handbook on Pastoral Ministry, Counseling and Leadership.* Grand Rapids: Zondervan, 1986.

Anderson, James D., and Ezra Earl Jones. *The Management of Ministry.* New York: Harper and Row, 1978.

Callahan, Kennon L. *Twelve Keys to an Effective Church.* San Francisco: Harper and Row, 1983.

Crabb, Lawrence J., Jr. *Understanding People: Deep Longings for Relationship.* Grand Rapids: Zondervan, 1987.

Fant, Clyde E. *Preaching for Today.* New York: Harper and Row, 1987.

Howard, J. Grant. *Creativity in Preaching.* Grand Rapids: Zondervan, 1987.

Huttenlocker, Keith. *Conflict and Caring: Preventing, Managing, and Resolving Conflict in the Church.* Grand Rapids: Zondervan, 1988.

Laney, Carl. *A Guide to Church Discipline.* Minneapolis: Bethany, 1985.

Lutzer, Erwin W. *Failure: The Back Door to Success.* Chicago: Moody, revised, 1976.

Richards, Lawrence O., and Clyde Hoeldtke. *A Theology of Church Leadership.* Grand Rapids: Zondervan, 1980.

Rush, Myron D. *Management: A Biblical Approach.* Wheaton, Ill.: Victor, 1983.

Schaller, Lyle E. *It's a Different World.* Nashville: Abingdon, 1987.

Smith, Fred. *Learning to Lead: How to Bring Out the Best in People.* Waco, Tex.: Word, 1986.

Stowe, Eugene L. *The Ministry of Shepherding.* Kansas City: Beacon Hill, 1976.

Thiessen, John Caldwell. *Pastoring the Smaller Church.* Grand Rapids: Zondervan, 1962.

Wagner, C. Peter. *Leading Your Church to Growth.* Ventura, Calif.: Regal, 1984.

Wiersbe, David, and Warren Wiersbe. *Making Sense of the Ministry.* Chicago: Moody, 1983.

Wiseman, Neil B. *Innovative Ideas for Pastors.* Kansas City: Beacon Hill, 1976.